Weekend Knitting Projects

Margaret Hubert
and
Dorothy Dean Gusick

VNR **VAN NOSTRAND REINHOLD COMPANY**
New York Cincinnati Toronto London Melbourne

**For Robert, Sharon, Mark,
Christopher, and Robert M.**
M.H.

For Richard, Robert, and David
D.D.G.

Photography by Christopher Hubert

The photograph on page 88 was taken by Bill Smith.

Copyright (c) 1979 by Litton Educational Publishing, Inc.
Library of Congress Catalog Card Number 79-12416
ISBN 0-442-23572-0

Printed in the United States of America
Design by Loudan Enterprises

Published in 1979 by Van Nostrand Reinhold Company
A division of Litton Educational Publishing, Inc.
135 West 50th Street, New York, NY 10020, U.S.A.

Van Nostrand Reinhold Limited
1410 Birchmount Road
Scarborough, Ontario M1P 2E7, Canada

Van Nostrand Reinhold Australia Pty. Ltd.
17 Queen Street
Mitcham, Victoria 3132, Australia

Van Nostrand Reinhold Company Limited
Molly Millars Lane
Wokingham, Berkshire, England

16 15 14 13 12 11 10 9 8 7 6 5 4 3

Library of Congress Cataloging in Publication Data
Hubert, Margaret.
  Weekend knitting projects.

  Includes index.
  1. Knitting. I. Gusick, Dorothy, joint author.
II. Title.
TT820'.H85   746.4'32   79-12416
ISBN 0-442-23572-0

Contents

Acknowledgments

When the final pages are typed, when all the corrections have been made and the "book" is finally finished, we begin to think about thanking all who helped make it possible.

Creating a book takes many hours of hard work. Naturally for working mothers, encouragement and understanding are a necessity. We sincerely wish to thank our families, without whom we could never have undertaken this project.

We also wish to thank Susan Rosenthal, who shaped and edited our work, and Nancy Green, editor-in-chief at Van Nostrand Reinhold. Both are a delight to work with.

Special thanks to Chris Hubert for his creative camera work and many hours of time, to Carmela Mancuso and Catherine Ghirardi for knitting some of the garments for us, to John Lawler for his advice and guidance, to the models for their time and patience, and to the yarn companies who donated their beautiful yarns for us to create with. Again, many thanks to all.

M. H. and D. D. G.

We wish to thank the following persons for modeling:

Priscilla Albrecht
Connie Bock
Carol Cardinale
Anita Cosenza
Mary Anne Cosenza
Gina De Antonio
Joan Fagan
Kevin Fagan
Philip Federico Jr.
Susan Fuirst
Lynn Gold
Stephen Gonda Jr.
Victoria Schrade Gonda
David Gusick
Richard Gusick
Robert Gusick

Robert Hubert Jr.
Sharon E. Hubert
Bernadette Lawler
Brian Lawler
Celeste Lawler
Clare Lawler
Louis Gunther Mancuso
Dana Mills
Darby Mills
Cathy Olmsted
Melissa Savino
William H.R. Shockey, Jr.
Geri Tacinelli
Ava Tang
Andrea Truppa
Rosalind Turner

Introduction

Some people think of knitting as an old-fashioned art, better suited to years gone by when life was slower. Women seldom worked outside their homes then, and there was more time to spend making hand-knits for family and friends. But, whether you are a busy executive, homemaker, or young mother with very few hours to yourself, you too can enjoy the great feeling of satisfaction that comes from creating something with your hands. You can turn out beautiful hand-knits in a minimum of hours. We call these projects "Weekenders," because, through the use of large needles and bulky yarns, you can literally complete one in a weekend.

These quick knits are ideally suited to our fast-paced modern life-style. Start a project on Friday and have a great-looking sweater, jacket, or hat and scarf to wear on Monday. Or, surprise a loved one with a gift that you have made yourself over the weekend. That is truly one of life's great pleasures, and you'll be amazed at how quickly these projects materialize before your very eyes.

Many of our projects require only the most basic knowledge of knitting. To make it even easier for the novice knitter we have tried to make our instructions as clear and simple as possible. There are no "shorthand" knitting abbreviations either. We think that instructions are much easier to read and understand when written out.

It's fun and exciting to create projects as beautiful as these in just a few hours. At first, you may want to follow our suggestions for yarn combinations exactly. But don't stop there. Be daring. Remember, on the jumbo needles everything is magnified. Even the elementary garter stitch, stockinette stitch, and rib stitch take on a new dimension when knitted in this manner. The beautiful yarns of today—homespun tweeds, chenilles, mohairs—come in an endless variety of wonderful textures and colors. By combining these yarns you are creating something unique . . . your very own. Do you need a jacket to match a "special" skirt? Start with a bulky yarn, add another color of knitting worsted, per-

haps a strand of mohair, and there you have it—a new yarn look of your own, an exclusive! Cast on about 12 stitches on a jumbo needle (we used #15, #17, and #19 needles most often), and knit a few rows. Does the gauge match ours? That's very important. Do you LOVE the way it looks? That's just as important. If not, pull it out and start again. Don't be afraid to try some off-beat colors, by the way. Sometimes the most unlikely combinations turn out the best. If you find it difficult to work with more than one skein at a time, roll the yarns together into one large ball.

Today's soaring price tags are one good reason for the fashion-conscious woman to try her hand at knitting. Anyone can turn out beautiful knitted clothes that rival those with a "designer" label . . . at a fraction of the price. With a little experience, a little confidence, and a few helpful tips from us, we hope that you will be able to design your own beautiful knits. Over the years, we have helped many women create great looking knits. Now, you can make them too, in a weekend.

The Proper Fit

Nothing beats the look of a well-made knit. But, no matter how well you knit, your end result will be spoiled if it does not fit properly. Before starting to knit any garment, be sure that you are making the correct size. Use the size needles indicated and the proper weight yarn. Check your work against the gauge. If it does not match, this means that you are knitting at a tension level different from ours. In that case, experiment with other sizes of knitting needles until your gauge matches ours.

Although each garment in the book was made with a specific yarn, a substitute can be used providing that it falls into the same weight class as the one we used. Make sure you are obtaining the same gauge with your substitute yarn that we did with ours or your garment will not turn out to be the size you planned.

To determine the person's correct size take body measurements at the fullest part of the chest, hips, and natural waistline. Then find the appropriate size on the chart given here. (Slight allowances have been added on for ease and proper fit.) Note that children's sizes are determined by the chest measurement and not age. Pick the size that is nearest to the chest measurement. Other adjustments can be made while you are working on the garment.

Standard Sizes and Measurements

Sizes

Misses and Women

	8	10	12	14	16	18
Bust	31½	32½	34	36	38	40
Waist	23	24	25½	27	29	31
Hips	33½	34½	36	38	40	42

Men

	34	36	38	40	42	44	46
Chest	34	36	38	40	42	44	46
Waist	30	32	34	36	38	40	42

Young Women and Men

	8	10	12	14	16
Chest	28	29	31	33	34
Waist	23	24	25	26	29
Hips	31	32	34	36	38

Children

	4	6	8	10	12	14
Chest	23	24	26	28	30	32
Waist	21	22	23½	24½	25½	26½
Hips	24	26	28	30	32	34

Infants and Toddlers

	6 mos	1	2	3	4
Chest	19	20	21	22	23
Waist	20	19½	20	20½	21
Hips	20	21	22	23	24
Height	22	25	29	31	33

The Language of Knitting

The terms that follow are important parts of a knitter's vocabulary. The list will serve as a crash course for the novice knitter and a refresher course for the more experienced.

Binding off should always be done in the pattern you are working loosely. To bind off work 2 stitches in pattern. Then with the left-hand needle, lift the first stitch worked over the second stitch, and drop off the needle. This makes 1 bound-off stitch. Work another stitch and repeat this procedure as required. If you are binding off completely, cut yarn when you come to the last stitch, leaving a 5-inch (12.5-cm) end, and bring cut end through the last stitch.

Changing colors is always done by picking up the color to be worked from underneath the dropped color. This method of work will prevent holes.

To *decrease,* unless otherwise specified, means to knit 2 stitches together as one.

Double-pointed needles are used for working rounds (no seams). They are sold in sets of four.

Garter stitch is done by knitting every row.

Gauge refers to the number of stitches and rows that make up 1 inch (2.5 cm) of knitted fabric. This is a most important factor in knitting garments that fit properly. All instructions are based upon an exact gauge.

To *increase,* unless otherwise specified, means to knit in the front of the stitch and leave it on the needle. Then knit in back of the same stitch and slip both stitches off the needle.

Joining yarn is done best at the outside edges of the garment, except when making a one-piece raglan. In that case, adding under the arm is best. You will have enough yarn to complete a row if the strand measures four times the width of the garment.

Placing a *marker* (may be either a commercially sold marker, a paper clip, or a piece of yarn tied into a little ring) on a needle is a means of marking a certain spot in your work. This marker is slipped from the left- to the right-hand needle as you work each row.

Multiple refers to the number of stitches worked to form 1 pattern. If you increase the number of stitches in a pattern, you must do so in the multiple.

Parentheses ( ) are used to enclose directions for larger sizes and also to indicate that the instructions enclosed within are to be repeated for a specific number of times.

Yarn over is a way to increase and is also used in delicate open-work patterns. When knitting, bring yarn under right-hand needle as if to purl and knit next stitch with the yarn in the purling position. To yarn over when purling wind yarn around right-hand needle once, then purl in the next stitch.

Picking up stitches is usually done along a piece already knitted. Always have the right side of the garment facing you. Using a crochet hook and a separate strand of yarn, pick up stitches, evenly spaced, along the edge of the work. As you work, slip the stitches off the back of the crochet hook onto your knitting needle. This takes a little practice. The idea is to pick up enough stitches so that there will be no holes in your work. Then increase or decrease to the amount of stitches needed and you will have a neat line of picked up stitches.

Ribbing is a combination of purling and knitting, as in knit 1, purl 1, or knit 2, purl 2. It is most often use for waistbands, cuffs, and neckbands because of its elastic quality.

Seed stitch, which is done with an odd number of stitches, means knit 1, purl 1 across the row, ending with knit 1. Row 1 is then repeated with the knit 1 over the purl 1 and the purl 1 over the knit 1.

To *sew seams together,* backstitching is the best method. Always pin right sides together, and take a running stitch with a backstitch about every ¼ inch.

Slip stitch means slip the stitch from the left-hand needle to the right-hand needle without working it. Then insert the right-hand needle as if to purl, unless otherwise specified.

Stockinette stitch is done by knitting 1 row, purling the next, and continuing in that fashion.

Helpful Hints for Weekend Knitters

In working with the very bulky yarns and jumbo needles we have found it necessary to "bend" the rules occasionally. The following tips will help you out.

• When sewing a shoulder seam, we sew from the right side, deliberately allowing the bound-off stitches to show. This forms a saddle shoulder effect (see photograph on page 13). This type of shoulder is much more comfortable to wear and lies better on these bulky sweaters. A conventional seam would be very thick and cumbersome.

• As far as blocking is concerned, we never block the very bulky sweaters. The loose, puffy quality of the patterns is their charm. Blocking would flatten and stretch the stitches out of shape.

• Whenever possible, the sleeves are picked up at the shoulder seam and worked downward. This eliminates another bulky seam and makes for a better-looking garment.

• When working with 2 or more strands of yarn, it is helpful to put each yarn in a separate bag. Keeping them separate as you work will avoid lots of tangles and will allow you to work at a faster pace and eliminate frazzled nerves also.

• Sew side seams using a backstitch, sewing very close to the edge of the stitch and making the narrowest seam possible.

• These garments are designed to be made quickly, with a minimum of finishing. Do not be afraid to experiment a little, changing patterns or colors to create your own individual look. You can always rip it out if you don't like what you've done without having wasted much time at all.

• To weave seams, where indicated, hold pieces to be joined side by side. Then, using an almost straight up-and-down motion (not overcast or backstitching), join the pieces together, keeping them as flat as possible.

• Many of the garments in this book are finished with crochet around the edges. Most are done with just 1 row of single crochet, some are done with 1 row of single crochet and then 1 row of backwards single crochet.

• To work single crochet on edges, always have right side of work facing you. In most cases, you should pick up every other stitch. Sometimes, if you have worked very tightly, you will have to pick up more often.

• To work backwards single crochet, work 1 row single crochet first; then, not turning the work, work single crochet from left to right over first row.

• To single crochet, yarn over hook, pick up a loop, yarn over hook, and pull through both loops on hook.

Woman's Mohair Stole
The simple pattern of this soft mohair stole is worked over
40 stitches for a length of 72 inches. You can watch it
grow right before your very eyes in a matter of a few hours.

Woman's Mohair Stole

See photograph on facing page.

Woman's Sizes
One size fits all.

Materials
11 skeins (1½ oz or 40g each) Majestic Mohair
  by Galler or any mohair to give gauge

Needles
#19
#10½ crochet hook

Gauge
2 stitches = 1 inch (2.5 cm)

Note: Yarn is used double strand throughout.
  This stole can be made into an afghan by
combining additional panels.

Pattern
Row 1 (right side): Purl 2, *knit 2 together,
yarn over, knit 2, purl 4, repeat from * ending
with knit 2 together, yarn over, knit 2, purl 2.
Row 2: Knit 2, *purl 2 together, yarn over, purl
2, knit 4, repeat from * ending with purl 2 together, yarn over, purl 2, knit 2. (See close-up
photograph.)

Stole
Cast on 40 stitches and work in pattern for 72
inches (180 cm), bind off loosely. Do not block.

Fringe
Cut yarn into 12-inch (30-cm) lengths. Hold 3
strands together, fold in half. With crochet
hook, draw folded loop through edges. Draw
strands through loop and tighten.

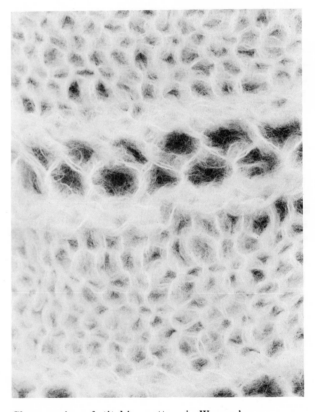

Close-up view of stitching pattern in Woman's
Mohair Stole.

Young Man's Seed-Stitch Pullover
This pullover is done entirely in seed stitch with a tweed yarn. The shawl-collar effect is achieved by ribbing a separate collar piece and sewing it to the sweater with an overlap.

Young Man's Seed-Stitch Pullover

See photograph on facing page.

Young Men's Sizes
Directions are for size 14. Changes for sizes 16 and 18 are in parentheses.

Materials
6 (6, 7) skeins (4 oz or 112g each) Donegal Tweed Homespun by Tahki or any tweed yarn to give gauge

Needles
#10
#11

Gauge
2 stitches = 1 inch (2.5 cm)

Note: Yarn is used double strand throughout.

Back
With #10 needles cast on 35 (37,39) stitches. Work ribbed waistband as follows:
Row 1: Knit 1 *purl 1, knit 1, repeat from * across row.
Row 2: Purl 1 *knit 1, purl 1, repeat from * across row.
Work even for 3 inches (7.5 cm). Change to #11 needles and work in seed stitch pattern as follows:
Row 1: Knit 1 *purl 1, knit 1, repeat from * across row.
Row 2: Same as Row 1.
Work even until 15½ (16, 16½) (38.8, 40, 41.3 cm) inches from beginning or desired length to underarm. At the beginning of the next 2 rows, bind off 2 stitches. Decrease 1 stitch each side, every other row, 3 times. Work in pattern until armhole measures 8 (8½, 9) inches (21.3, 22.5, 23.8 cm). At the beginning of the next 4 rows, bind off 4 (4, 4) stitches. Bind off remaining stitches.

Front
Cast on 35 (37, 39) stitches and work same as Back to underarm. At the beginning of the next 2 rows, bind off 2 stitches. Work across 13 (14, 15) stitches, join new yarn. Bind off center 5 stitches and work remaining 13 (14, 15) stitches. Work both sides, shaping arm side as back, and, at the same time, decreasing neck edge every 6th row, 2 (3, 4) times. Work until armhole measures 8 (8½, 9) inches (20, 21.3, 22.5 cm), and bind off 4 (4, 4) stitches from each arm side, twice.

Collar
With #10 needles, cast on 70 (74, 78) stitches. Work in knit 1, purl 1 ribbing for 3 inches (7.5 cm), bind off loosely.

Sleeves
With #10 needles, cast on 17 (19, 21) stitches. Work in ribbing pattern for 3 inches (7.5 cm), change to #11 needles. Increase 1 stitch each side and work even in seed stitch pattern for 7 (8, 9) inches (17.5, 20, 22.5 cm). Increase 1 stitch each side, every 2 inches (5 cm), 4 times. Work even until piece measures 18 (18½, 19) inches (45, 46.3, 48 cm) from beginning or desired length to underarm. At the beginning of the next 2 rows, decrease 2 stitches. Decrease 1 stitch each side, every other row, until 5 stitches remain, bind off remaining stitches.

Finishing
Sew shoulder seams. Sew in collar band, overlapping at front edge with left side on top. Sew up side seams. Sew sleeve seams and sew into garment. Do not block.

Woman's Cuddly Pullover With Shawl Collar
Done in a simple stockinette stitch, this lovely sweater is
set off by the chenille yarn used for the body and the worsted
yarn for the waistband, collar, and cuffs. The shawl collar
is made separately and then sewn on.

Woman's Cuddly Pullover With Shawl Collar

See photograph on facing page.

Women's Sizes
Directions are for small size. Changes for medium and large sizes are in parentheses.

Materials
8 (8, 9) skeins (1¾ oz or 50 g each) Chenille by Galler or any chenille to give gauge
2 (2, 3) skeins (3½ oz or 100 g each) knitting worsted

Needles
#10
#11

Gauge
2 stitches = 1 inch (2.5 cm)

Back
Using a double strand of knitting worsted and #10 needles, cast on 38 (40, 42) stitches. Knit 1, purl 1 in ribbing for 3 inches (7.5 cm). Break worsted and join 1 strand of chenille. Using #11 needles, knit 1 row, purl 1 row in stockinette stitch till 15 (15, 16) inches (37.5, 37.5, 40 cm) from beginning. At the beginning of the next 2 rows, bind off 2 stitches. Work even till armhole measures 6½ inches (16.3 cm). Work across next 13 stitches, join new strand of chenille yarn, bind off center 12 (14, 16) stitches, work remaining 13 stitches. Working both sides at once, decrease 1 stitch each neck edge, every row, 3 times. Work even till armhole is 8 (8½, 9) inches (20, 21.3, 22.5 cm). Bind off remaining stitches.

Front
Work same as Back, except start neck shaping at 4½ inches (11.3 cm) from start of armhole. Work even to shoulder and bind off. Sew shoulder seam from right side, forming a saddle shoulder (See photograph.)

Sleeves
Using 1 strand of chenille yarn and #11 needles, pick up 28 (30, 32) stitches along armhole, being sure stitches are divided equally on each side of shoulder seam. Knit 1 row, purl 1 row in stockinette stitch for 18 (18½, 19) inches (45, 46.3, 47.5 cm). Changing to #10 needles and a double strand of worsted, decrease evenly across 1 row to 22 (24, 26) stitches. Knit 1, purl 1 in ribbing for 3 inches (7.5 cm). Bind off in ribbing.

Collar
With #10 needles and a double strand of knitting worsted, cast on 120 (124, 128) stitches. Working in knit 1, purl 1 ribbing, decrease 1 stitch each side, every row, till collar is 6 inches (15 cm) wide in center. Bind off.

Finishing
Sew collar in place, overlapping the front edges along the bound-off center stitches. Sew underarm seams. Do not block.

Close-up view of how a saddle shoulder looks when completed.

Woman's Curly Battle Jacket

Woman's Curly Battle Jacket
This jacket is done predominantly in a curly yarn. Perfect for fall or spring, it can be put together as easily as a basic cardigan.

Women's Sizes
Directions are for small size. Changes for medium and large sizes are in parentheses.

Materials
3 (3, 3) skeins (3½ oz or 100 g each) Vail Homespun by Brunswick or any bulky yarn to give gauge
10 (10, 10) skeins (2 oz or 56 g each) Curlama by Stanley Berocco or any curly yarn to give gauge
1 heavy-duty separating zipper

Needles
#15
#17
#10½ crochet hook

Gauge
2 stitches = 1 inch (2.5 cm)

Note: Vail yarn is used double strand for waistband, collar, and cuffs, Curlama is used double strand for body of jacket.
Purl side is the right side.

Back
With #15 needles and Vail yarn, cast on 34 (36, 38) stitches. Knit 1, purl 1 in ribbing for 3½ inches (8.8 cm). Changing to #17 needles and Curlama, work stockinette stitch (knit 1 row, purl 1 row) until 14 (15, 16) inches (35, 37.5, 40 cm) from beginning, ending on a purl row. At the beginning of the next 2 rows, bind off 2 stitches. Work even till armhole is 8 (8½, 9) inches (20, 21.3, 22.5 cm). At the beginning of the next 2 rows, bind off 10 stitches. Place remaining stitches on a holder.

Left Front

With #15 needles and Vail, cast on 17 (18, 19) stitches. Knit 1, purl 1 in ribbing for 3½ inches (8.8 cm). Changing to #17 needles and Curlama, work in stockinette stitch till armhole. At arm side, bind off 2 stitches. Work even till armhole measures 6 (6½, 7) inches (15, 16.3, 17.5 cm), ending at front edge. At front edge, place 3 (4, 5) stitches on a holder. Decrease 1 stitch at neck edge, every row, twice. Work even to shoulder. Bind off.

Right Front

Work same as Left Front, reversing shaping.

Sleeves

Sew shoulder seams, with right side facing you. With #17 needles and Curlama, pick up 26 (28, 30) stitches along armhole. Work even in stockinette stitch till 18 (19, 20) inches (45, 47.5, 50.5 cm). On last row, decrease evenly across row to 18 (20, 20) stitches. Changing to #15 needles and Vail, knit 1, purl 1 in ribbing for 3 inches (7.5 cm). Bind off in ribbing. Sew underarm seams. With #15 needles and Vail, with right side facing you, pick up 38 (40, 42) stitches along neck edge, including stitches on holders. Knit 1, purl 1 in ribbing for 2 inches (5 cm). Change to #17 needles and continue in ribbing for 3 inches (7.5 cm) more. Bind off in ribbing.

Finishing

Using #10½ crochet hook and Vail, work 1 row single crochet along each front edge. Sew in zipper. Do not block.

Woman's Curly Battle Jacket done in a combination of Knob Tweed and Cozy yarns by Unger for a totally different effect. To work the sweater in this way follow the instructions and gauge of the curly jacket. Use one strand of Knob tweed and one strand of Cozy held together throughout. The needles will be the same. You will need 6 skeins (2 ounces or 56 grams each) of Cozy and 11 skeins of Knob Tweed.

Seed-Stitch Hat and Scarf Set

Sizes
One size fits all.

Materials
4 skeins (4 oz or 112 g each) Bulky by Spinnerin or any bulky yarn to give gauge

Needles
#17

Gauge
2 stitches = 1 inch (2.5 cm)

Note: Yarn is used double strand throughout.

Pattern
*Knit 1, purl 1, repeat from * across row.

Hat

With #17 needles, cast on 31 stitches. Work pattern for 12 inches (30 cm). On next row, knit 2 together across row. Break yarn, leaving a long end. Pull this end through remaining stitches, gather up, weave seam. Fold bottom up once or twice as desired for cuff. Do not block.

Scarf

With #17 needles, cast on 15 stitches. Work in pattern for 72 inches (180 cm). Bind off in pattern. Cut yarn in 12-inch (30-cm) lengths and fringe each end. Do not block.

Seed-Stitch Hat and Scarf Set
With 4 skeins of yarn and some large knitting needles, you can complete a hat and scarf set in no time at all.

Rib-Stitch Hat and Scarf Set

Sizes
One size fits all.

Materials
4 skeins (4 oz or 112 g each) Bulky by Spinnerin
or any bulky yarn to give gauge

Needles
#17

Gauge
2 stitches = 1 inch (2.5 cm)

Note: Yarn is used double strand throughout.

Pattern
*Knit 1, purl 1, repeat from * across row.

Hat

With #17 needles, cast on 40 stitches. Work
pattern for 12 inches (30 cm). On next row, knit
2 together across row. Break yarn, leaving a
long end. Pull this end through remaining
stitches, gather up, weave seam. Fold bottom
up one or twice as desired for cuff. Do not block.

Scarf

With #17 needles, cast on 20 stitches. Work in
pattern for 72 inches (180 cm). Bind off in
pattern. Cut yarn in 12-inch (30-cm) lengths
and fringe each end. Do not block.

Rib-Stitch Hat and Scarf Set
Hat and scarf sets like this one make fine gifts. During the
holiday season, when time is so precious, this might be
just the solution you're looking for.

Reversible Baby Blanket
A simple baby blanket, such as this one, is done by knitting across one row, knitting 1, purling 1, knitting 1, across the next, and so on. This simple pattern creates a ribbed effect on one side and a nubbed texture on the reverse side.

Reversible Baby Blanket

See photograph on facing page.

Size
One size—25 by 36 inches (62.5 by 90 cm)

Materials
6 skeins (3½ oz or 100 g each) Windrush by
  Brunswick or any worsted yarn to give gauge

Needles
#17

Gauge
2 stitches = 1 inch (2.5 cm)

Note: Yarn is used 4 strands held together
throughout.

Pattern
Row 1: Knit across row.
Row 2: Knit 1, *purl 1, knit 1, repeat from *
across row. (See photographs for views of both
sides of blanket.)

Blanket
With #17 needles, cast on 50 stitches. Work
pattern till blanket is 36 inches (90 cm) long.

Finishing
Bind off. Cut remaining yarn into 12-inch (30-
cm) lengths. Holding 3 strands together, place
fringe every other stitch all around blanket.

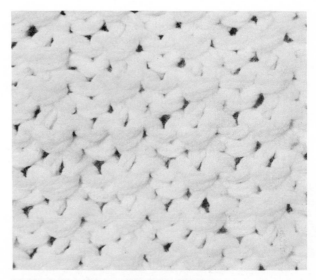

Nubbed side of Reversible Baby Blanket

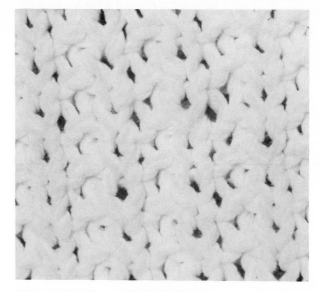

Ribbed side of Reversible Baby Blanket.

Plaid Baby Afghan
This blanket consists of five strips of alternating dark and light color boxes.

Plaid
Baby Afghan

See photograph on facing page.

Size
One size—approximately 36 by 50 inches (90 by 125 cm)

Materials
10 skeins (2 oz or 56 g each) Bulky Nantuck by Columbia Minerva in Color A or any bulky yarn to give gauge
10 skeins in Color B

Needles
#17
#10½ crochet hook

Gauge
2 stitches = 1 inch (2.5 cm)

Note: Yarn is used double strand throughout.

Pattern
Row 1: Knit across row.
Row 2: Purl 7, knit 1, purl 7.

Strip 1 (make 3):
With 2 strands of Color A, cast on 15 stitches. Work in pattern till 16 rows are completed, break Color A. Join Color B, and repeat pattern for 16 rows. Continue to alternate Color A and Color B till 7 color boxes are completed, ending with Color A.

Strip 2 (make 2):
Starting with Color B, repeat the pattern, alternating Colors A and B. Follow same pattern till 7 color boxes are completed, ending with Color B.

Finishing
Before sewing strips together, using 1 strand of each color and a number 10½ crochet hook, work 1 row single crochet over the garter stitch line in the center of each strip. (See photograph.) This row must be worked very loosely. Now sew strips together. Fringe top and bottom, using 2 strands of each color in every other stitch along edges. Do not block.

Close-up of Plaid Baby Afghan.

Infant's Two-Colored Sweatshirt
Done in reverse stockinette stitch, this two-colored, happy pullover is perfect for toddlers. It's a good idea to make sleeves longer than necessary on infants' clothing. They can always be rolled up neatly and rolled down when the need arises—and it will!

Infant's Two-Colored Sweatshirt

See photograph on facing page.

Infants' Sizes
Directions are for size 1. Changes for sizes 2 and 3 are in parentheses.

Materials
2 skeins (3½ oz or 100 g each) bulky yarn in Color A
2 skeins in Color B

Needles
#13
#15
#10½ crochet hook

Gauge
2½ stitches = 1 inch (2.5 cm)

Note: Yarn is used double strand throughout.

Back
With #13 needles, cast on 24 (26, 30) stitches with Color A. Knit 1, purl 1 in ribbing for 2 inches (5 cm). Changing to #15 needles and Color B, work reverse stockinette stitch (purl 1 row, knit 1 row) for 2 rows. Work 2 rows in Color A, and then continue in Color B till 7 (7½, 8) inches (17.5, 18.8, 20 cm) from beginning. Mark for armholes and work for 4 (4½, 5) inches (10, 11.3, 12.5 cm) more. At the beginning of the next 2 rows, bind off 7 (8, 8) stitches. Place remaining stitches on holder.

Front
Work same as Back till 5 (5½, 6) inches (12.5, 13.8, 15 cm) from beginning. Work across 10 (11, 13) stitches, join new yarn, bind off center 4 stitches, work remaining 10 (11, 13) stitches. Continue working both sides. Mark armholes at proper place and continue to work till 2 (2½, 3) inches (5, 6.3, 7.5 cm) above armhole marker. At front edges, place 2 stitches on holders, then decrease neck edge 1 (1, 2,) time. Work even to shoulder, bind off.

Sleeves
Sew shoulder, pick up 24 (26, 30) stitches along armhole with Color A. Work 2 rows in Color A, 2 rows in Color B, and finish sleeve in Color A. Work till 7 (8, 9) inches (17.5, 20, 22.5 cm), decreasing 4 stitches along 1 row. Change to #13 needles, knit 1, purl 1 in ribbing for 2 inches. Bind off in ribbing. With Color A and #15 needles, pick up 30 (32, 34) stitches along neck edge for hood, including stitches on holders. Work even in reverse stockinette stitch for 8½ (9, 10) inches (21.3, 22.5, 25 cm). Bind off.

Finishing
Sew top hood seam. Sew underarm seams. With Color B work 1 row single crochet along front edges and around hood. With Color A work 1 row single crochet around front edges and hood. With Color A make 2 small chains for ties and attach at neck at base of hood. Do not block.

Striped Christmas Stocking

Materials
1 skein (2 oz or 56 g) bulky yarn in red
1 skein bulky yarn in white

Needles
#17
#10½ crochet hook

Gauge
2 stitches = 1 inch (2.5 cm)

Stocking
With #17 needles, cast on 20 stitches with red yarn. Knit every row, alternating 2 rows red, 2 rows white, till there are 10 stripes in all. Break off yarn. Place 7 stitches on a holder, join yarn, and knit center 6 stitches, place last 7 stitches on a holder. Continue in the striping pattern on center 6 stitches, work till 4 more stripes are completed. Place the first 7 stitches held onto free needle, join red yarn, and knit these stitches. Pick up and knit 4 stitches along side of instep place marker (4 stripes added in center), knit across instep, place marker, pick up and knit 4 along other side, knit remaining 7 stitches from holder. Continue with red yarn, working in garter stitch (knit each row). Work 1 row, then decrease 1 stitch before and after each marker (4 decreases). Work 3 rows even, repeat the decrease row. Work 1 row even, bind off.

Striped Christmas Stocking
This can be the start of a new tradition at your home. Too busy to knit a stocking? The next time you're watching the TV Movie of the Week, grab some yarn and needles. You'll be done before the plot has thickened.

Finishing
Sew back seam. With white yarn, work 1 row single crochet around top edge. Work 1 row loop stitch. Repeat last 2 rows till 3 loop rows have been worked, end off..

To make loop stitch: (wrong side of work), start to work as for single crochet, wind yarn around finger 2 times, catch both strands, then complete stitch as for single crochet.

Granny Bag

Size
One size.

Materials
4 skeins (2 oz or 56 g each) Aspen Bulky by
Brunswick or any bulky yarn to give gauge
1 set of round bamboo handles, 6-inch (15-cm)
or any suitable set of handles

Needles
#15
#10½ crochet hook

Gauge
2½ stitches = 1 inch (2.5 cm)

Note: Yarn is used double strand throughout.

Back
Cast on 25 stitches. Knit 1, *purl 1, knit 1, repeat
from * across row. Continue in pattern for 12
inches (30 cm). Bind off in pattern.

Front
Work same as Back.

Finishing
Holding 2 pieces together, using 1 strand of
yarn and number 10½ crochet hook, and starting at top right side, work 1 row of single
crochet through both thicknesses around 3
sides, leaving top open. Do not break yarn.
Continue working single crochet on 1 front and
over 1 handle. Repeat same on other side. Do
not block.

Granny Bag
The circulor bamboo handles give an unusual look to
this easy-to-make bag.

25

Basketweave-Stitch Bag
Bags are fun and easy to make and are great for gift giving, as well. This basketweave-stitch bag with its thick cord handle would be a good bazaar item also.

Basketweave-Stitch Bag

See photograph on facing page.

Size
One size.

Materials
4 skeins (3½ oz or 100 g each) Nevada or any
   bulky yarn to give gauge
2 straight wooden handles with knob ends,
   12-inch (30-cm)

Needles
#17
double-pointed bulky cable needles
#10½ crochet hook

Gauge
2 stitches = 1 inch (2.5 cm)

Note: Yarn is worked double strand throughout.

Pattern
Row 1: Knit across row.
Row 2: Purl across row.
Row 3: * Slip next 3 stitches onto cable needle,
hold to back, knit next 3 stitches, knit 3 stitches
from cable needle, repeat from * to end of row.
Row 4: Purl across row.
Row 5: Knit across row.
Row 6: Purl across row.
Row 7: Knit 3, * slip next 3 stitches onto cable
needle, hold to front, knit next 3 stitches, knit 3
stitches from cable needle, repeat from * to
last 3 stitches, knit 3.
Row 8: Purl across row.

Bag
With #17 needles, cast on 72 stitches. Work even
in basketweave pattern for 17 inches (42.5 cm),
bind off.

Finishing
Fold bag in half lengthwise. Sew side seams,
leaving 3 inches (7.5 cm) open at top on each
side. Work 1 row single crochet around top and
open sides, pulling in slightly along top edges.
Holding handle in place, work 1 row single
crochet to attach bag to handle.

Make 2 shoulder straps as follows: Cut 6
strands of yarn each 160 inches (40 cm) long
and fold in half. Anchor looped end. Twist
together until very tightly wound. Bring both
ends together, hold, let cord twist naturally.
Tie loose ends securely to handles.

Woman's Fisherman's Knit Pullover
Here's a perfect sporty pullover that is suitable for a man
or a woman. The pattern is a simple repetition of eight rows.

Woman's Fisherman's Knit Pullover

See photograph on facing page. This sweater can also be made for a young man. See directions on page 31.

Women's Sizes
Directions are for small size. Changes for medium and large sizes are in parentheses.

Materials
10 (12, 14) skeins (4 oz or 112 g each) Bulky by Spinnerin or any bulky yarn to give gauge

Needles
#15
#17

Gauge
2 stitches = 1 inch (2.5 cm)

Note: Yarn is used double strand throughout.

Pattern
Row 1: Knit across row.
Row 2: Purl 4 (5, 6), knit 1, *purl 4, knit 1, repeat from * 4 times, ending with purl 4 (5, 6).
Row 3: Work same as Row 1.
Row 4: Work same as Row 2.
Row 5: Work same as Row 1.
Row 6: Work same as Row 2.
Row 7: Knit across row.
Row 8: Knit across row.

Back
With #15 needles, cast on 34 (36, 38) stitches. Knit 1, purl 1 in ribbing for 3 inches (7.5 cm). Change to #17 needles and work pattern till 14 (15, 16) inches (35, 37.5, 40 cm) or desired length to underarm. At the beginning of the next 2 rows, bind off 2 stitches. Work even till armhole measures 7½ (8, 8½) inches (18.8, 20, 21.3 cm). At the beginning of the next 2 rows, bind off 10 stitches. Place remaining stitches on holder.

Front
Work same as Back till armhole measures 5½ (6, 6½) inches (13.8, 15, 16.3 cm). Work across 12 stitches, place center 6 (8, 10) stitches on holder, join new yarn, and work remaining 12 stitches. Working both sides at once, each with separate strands of yarn, decrease 1 stitch each neck edge, every row, 2 times. Work even to shoulder, bind off remaining 10 stitches.

Sleeves
Sew 1 shoulder, pick up 24 (26, 28) stitches for Sleeve and work in pattern, decreasing 1 stitch each side, every 4 inches (10 cm), 3 times. Work even till 16 (17, 18) inches (40, 42.5, 45 cm) or desired length. Change to #15 needles, knit 1, purl 1 in ribbing for 3 inches (7.5 cm). Bind off in ribbing. Work neckband before sewing other shoulder as follows: With #15 needles, pick up 34 (36, 38) stitches around neck, including stitches on holders. Knit 1, purl 1 in ribbing for 4 rows. Bind off in ribbing. Sew other shoulder and work other sleeve to correspond.

Finishing
Sew underarm seams. Do not block.

Young Man's Fisherman's Knit Pullover
Here is one of those sweaters that looks great on men or women. For women's directions see page 29.

Young Man's Fisherman's Knit Pullover

See photograph on facing page. This sweater can also be made for a woman. See directions on page 29.

Young Men's Sizes

Directions are for size 12. Changes for sizes 14 and 16 are in parentheses.

Materials

8 (10, 12) skeins (4 oz or 112 g each) Bulky by Spinnerin or any bulky yarn to give gauge

Needles

#15
#17

Gauge

2 stitches = 1 inch

Note: Yarn is used double strand throughout.

Pattern

Row 1: Knit across row.
Row 2: Purl 3 (4, 5), knit 1, *purl 4, knit 1, repeat from * 4 times, ending with purl 3 (4, 5).
Row 3: Work same as Row 1.
Row 4: Work same as Row 2.
Row 5: Work same as Row 1.
Row 6: Work same as Row 2.
Row 7: Knit across row.
Row 8: Knit across row.

Back

With #15 needles cast on 32 (34, 36) stitches. Knit 1, purl 1 in ribbing for 2 inches. Change to #17 needles and work pattern till 13 (14, 15) inches (32.5, 35, 37.5 cm) or desired length to underarm. At the beginning of the next 2 rows, bind off 2 stitches. Work even till armhole measures 7 (7½, 8) inches (17.5, 18.8, 20 cm). At the beginning of the next 2 rows, bind off 10 stitches. Place remaining stitches on holder.

Front

Work same as Back till armhole measures 5 (5½, 6) inches (12.5, 13.8, 15 cm). Work across 12 stitches, place center 4 (6, 8) stitches on holder, join new yarn, and work remaining 12 stitches. Working both sides at once, each with separate strands of yarn, decrease 1 stitch each neck edge, every row, 2 times. Work even to shoulder, bind off remaining 10 stitches.

Sleeves

Sew 1 shoulder, pick up 22 (24, 26) stitches for sleeve and work in pattern, decreasing 1 stitch each side, every 4 inches (10 cm) 3 times. Work even till 16 (17, 18) inches (40, 42.5, 45 cm) or desired length. Change to #15 needles, knit 1, purl 1 in ribbing for 2 inches. Bind off in ribbing. Work neckband before sewing other shoulder as follows: With #15 needles, pick up 32 (34, 36) stitches around neck, including stitches on holders. Knit 1, purl 1 in ribbing for 4 rows. Bind off in ribbing. Sew other shoulder and work other Sleeve to correspond. (See close-up photograph of shoulder.)

Finishing

Sew underarm seams. Do not block.

Woman's Warm-Up Cardigan

See photograph on facing page.

Women's Sizes
Directions are for small size. Changes for medium and large sizes are in parentheses.

Materials
6 (6, 7) skeins (4 oz or 112 g each) Big Berella Bulky by Bernat, in Color A or any bulky yarn to give gauge
2 skeins in Color B
1 skein in Color C
heavy-duty separating zipper

Needles
#15
#17
#10½ crochet hook
3 large stitch holders

Gauge
1½ stitches = 1 inch (2.5 cm)

Note: Yarn is used double strand throughout.

Ribbing Pattern
Row 1: Knit across row.
Row 2: Knit 1, purl 1 across row.

Back
With #15 needles and Color B, cast on 32 (34, 36) stitches. Work in ribbing pattern for 8 rows. Change to Color C and work for 6 rows. Change back to Color B and work for 8 rows. Change to Color A and, with #17 needles, work in stockinette stitch (knit 1 row, purl 1 row) for 14½ (15, 15½) inches (36.3, 37.5, 38.8 cm) from beginning or desired length to underarm. At the beginning of the next 2 rows, bind off 2 stitches. Work even till armhole measures 8 (8½, 9) inches (20, 21.3, 22.5 cm). At the beginning of the next 2 rows, bind off 4 (5, 5) stitches. At the beginning of the next 2 rows, bind off 5 (5, 6) stitches. Place remaining stitches on a stitch holder.

Left Front
With #15 needles and Color B, cast on 16 (17, 18) stitches and work colors and pattern as Back. Change to #17 needles and Color A. Work in stockinette stitch for 2 rows. Work pocket as follows: Work 6 (7, 8) stitches and place remaining 10 stitches on holder. Cast 10 stitches onto needle and work in stockinette stitch for 5 inches (12.5 cm), ending at front edge. Bind off 10 stitches and place remaining 6 (7, 8) stitches on holder. Place the 10 stitches previously held onto needle and work in stockinette stitch for 5 inches (12.5 cm), ending at inside edge. Now slip the 6 (7, 8) stitches that are on the holder onto the needle and continue in one piece until the work measures 14½ (15, 15½) inches (36.3, 37.5, 38.8 cm) to match Back. At arm side, bind off 2 stitches and work even until arm measures 6½ (7, 8) inches (16.3, 17.5, 20 cm). Shape neck as follows: On the knit side, knit to end of row and place last 4 stitches of neck edge on stitch holder. Decrease 1 stitch at neck edge, next 3 rows. At the beginning of the next 2 rows, bind off 4 (5, 5) stitches. Bind off remaining stitches.

Right Front
Work same as Left Front, reversing pocket, arm, and neck shapings.

Woman's Warm-Up Cardigan
Perfect for early spring and late fall, this sporty jacket is done in a simple stockinette stitch. The side pockets are done by placing stitches on a holder and increasing. The sweater looks beautiful in three colors or in one solid color.

Collar

Sew shoulder seams together. With #15 needles and right side facing you, pick up 30 stitches around neckline, including stitches from holders and across back of neck. Using Color B, work in ribbing pattern for 4 rows. Reverse ribbing and work for 4 more rows. Change to #17 needles and work in Color C for 6 rows. Change to Color B and work for 7 rows, bind off loosely.

Sleeves

With #17 needles and Color A, pick up 23 (24, 25) stitches. Work in stockinette stitch for 9 inches (22.5 cm). Decrease 1 stitch each side, every inch (2.5 cm), 3 times. Change to #15 needles and Color B, and work next 8 rows in ribbing pattern. Work next 6 rows in Color C, next 8 rows in Color B, bind off.

Finishing

Join side and sleeve seams. Sew pockets in place. Work 1 row of single crochet down center fronts of garment. Sew in heavy-duty separating zipper.

Young Man's Tweed Zippered Cardigan
Done in reverse stockinette stitch with tweed yarn, this
sweater is accented with stripes at the shoulder.

Young Man's Tweed Zippered Cardigan

See photograph on facing page.

Young Men's Sizes

Directions are for size 12. Changes for sizes 14 and 16 are in parentheses.

Materials

10 (11, 12) skeins (1¾ oz or 50 g each) Eskimo Special Tweed by Galler in Color A or any tweed yarn to give gauge
2 skeins in Color B
2 skeins in Color C
heavy-duty separating zipper

Needles

#13
#15
#J or #10 crochet hook

Gauge

2½ stitches = 1 inch (2.5 cm)

Note: Yarn is used double strand throughout.

Back

With #13 needles and Color A, cast on 40 (42, 44) stitches. Knit 1, purl 1 in ribbing for 3 inches (7.5 cm). Change to #15 needles and work in reverse stockinette stitch (purl 1 row, knit 1 row) till 13 (14, 15) inches (32.5, 35, 37.5 cm) or desired length to armhole. At the beginning of the next 2 rows, bind off 2 stitches. Decrease 1 stitch each side, every other row, 2 times. Work even till armhole measures 4½ (5, 5½) inches (11.3, 12.5, 13.8 cm). Work 2 rows in Color B, 2 rows in Color A, 2 rows in Color C, 2 rows in Color A, 2 rows in Color B. At the beginning of the next 2 rows, bind off 10 (11, 11) stitches. Place remaining stitches on holder.

Left Front

Cast on 20 (21, 22) stitches. Work same as Back till armhole measures 4½ (5, 5½) inches (11.3, 12.5, 13.8 cm). While working striping pattern as on Back, place 4 stitches at front edge on holder. Decrease neck edge every row, 2 (2, 3) times. Complete striping pattern, bind off remaining stitches.

Right Front

Work same as Left Front, reversing shaping.

Sleeves

With #13 needles, cast on 22 (24, 24) stitches. Work in knit 1, purl 1 ribbing for 3 inches (7.5 cm). Change to #15 needles. Work in reverse stockinette stitch, increasing 1 stitch each side, every 3 inches (7.5 cm), 3 (4, 4) times. Work even till 16 (17, 18) inches (40, 42.5, 45 cm) or desired length. At the beginning of the next 2 rows, bind off 2 stitches. Decrease 1 stitch each side, every other row, till 8 stitches remain, bind off.

Pockets

Cast on 14 (16, 16) stitches. Work in reverse stockinette stitch for 4 inches (10 cm), bind off. Make 4 pockets altogether.

Finishing

Sew shoulders. With #13 needle, pick up 40 (42, 44) stitches around neck, including stitches on holders. Knit 1, purl 1 in ribbing for 3 inches (7.5 cm), bind off. Fold neckband in half and sew to inside for double collar. Sew remaining seams. Work 1 row single crochet around each pocket and sew in place. Work 1 row single crochet around front edges. Sew in heavy-duty zipper. Do not block.

Girl's Classic Skirt and Top Set
The decorative holes at the bottom edges of the skirt and top are done by yarning over and knitting 2 together across the row. For another view of the skirt and its top see page 38.

Girl's Classic Skirt and Top Set

See photograph on facing page.

Girl's Sizes
Directions are for size 2. Changes for sizes 4 and 6 are in parentheses.

Materials
4 (5, 6) skeins (4 oz or 112 g each) Big Berella Bulky by Bernat or any bulky yarn to give gauge
2 large buttons
24-inch (60-cm) length of ½-inch elastic

Needles
#15
#10½ crochet hook

Gauge
5 stitches = 2 inches (5 cm)

Top

Back
With #15 needles, cast on 28 (30, 32) stitches. Knit 1 row, purl 1 row. Next row, knit 1 *yarn over, knit 2 together, repeat from * across row, ending the row with knit 1. Continue in stockinette stitch (knit 1 row, purl 1 row) till 7 (8, 9) inches (17.5, 20, 22.5 cm) from beginning. At the beginning of the next 2 rows, bind off 2 stitches. Decrease 1 stitch each side, every other row, 2 times. Work even till 3½ (4, 4½) inches (8.8, 10, 11.3 cm) from armhole. Work across 7 stitches, join new ball of yarn, bind off center 6 (8, 10) stitches, work remaining 7 stitches. Working both sides at once with separate balls of yarn, decrease neck edges every other row, 2 times. Work even for 3 (4, 5) inches (7.5, 10, 12.5 cm), ending on a purl row. Next row, knit 2 together, knit 1, knit 2 together. Next row, purl 3 together, end off.

Front
Work same as Back till both neck decreases are completed. Work even for 2 (3, 4) inches (5, 7.5, 10 cm), then complete point as on Back.

Finishing
Sew side seams. Starting at right underarm seam, work 1 row single crochet around entire upper edge of garment, making a buttonloop, by chaining 3, skipping 1, at each Back tab point. Work 1 row single crochet around bottom. Using a double strand of yarn, make a chain, about 30 inches (75 cm) long. Weave this chain in and out of yarn over spaces at bottom for tie. Block by steaming gently with a pressing cloth, wrong side out. Sew 2 buttons in place on front tabs.

Skirt

Back
With #15 needles, cast on 30 (32, 34) stitches. Work in stockinette stitch same as for Top till 2 (3, 3) inches (5, 7.5, 7.5 cm) from beginning. Decrease 1 stitch each side and repeat this decrease every 2 inches (5 cm) 2 (3, 4) times more. Work even till 9 (10, 11) inches (22.5, 25, 27.5 cm) or desired length, bind off.

Front
Work same as Back.

Finishing
Sew side seams. Work 1 row single crochet around bottom edge of Skirt. Work 1 row single crochet around top of Skirt. Do not break yarn. Holding ½-inch (1.25-cm) elastic in place, work a 2nd row of single crochet around elastic, end off. Adjust elastic to proper waist size and sew. Block by steaming gently with a pressing cloth, wrong side out.

Girl's Classic Coat and Hat Set
This little girl's coat can be made just like a cardigan—
only longer. Directions for the skirt and top are on page 37.

Girl's Classic Coat and Hat Set

See photograph on facing page.

Girls' Sizes
Directions are for size 4. Changes for sizes 6 and 8 are in parentheses.

Materials
8 (9, 9) skeins (4 oz or 112 g each) Big Berella Bulky by Bernat or any bulky yarn to give gauge

Needles
#19
#10½ crochet hook

Gauge
1½ stitches = 1 inch (2.5 cm)

Note: Yarn is used double strand throughout.

Coat

Back
With #19 needles, cast on 28 (30, 32) stitches. Work in stockinette stitch (knit 1 row, purl 1 row), decreasing 1 stitch each side of work every 4 inches (10 cm), 2 times. Work even till 14 (15, 16) inches (35, 37.5, 40 cm) or desired length to armhole. At the beginning of the next 2 rows, bind off 2 stitches. Work even till armhole measures 6 (6½, 7) inches (15, 16.3, 17.5 cm). At the beginning of the next 2 rows, bind off 6 (6, 7) stitches. Bind off remaining stitches.

Left Front
Cast on 16 (17, 18) stitches. Work in stockinette stitch, decreasing arm sides same as Back. Work to armhole. Shape armhole as Back, and, at the same time, decrease 1 stitch each neck edge, every other row, till 6 (6, 7) stitches remain. Work even till shoulder, bind off.

Right Front
Work same as Left Front, reversing shaping.

Sleeves
Cast on 14 stitches. Work in stockinette stitch, increasing 1 stitch each side, every 4 inches (10 cm), 1 (2, 2) time. Work even till 11 (12, 13) inches (27.5, 30, 32.5 cm) or desired length to underarm, bind off loosely.

Finishing
Sew seams. Work 1 row of single crochet and 1 row of backward single crochet around entire outside edge of coat and also around sleeves. Sew on buttons, using spaces in crochet edges as buttonholes.

Hat

With #19 needles, cast on 26 (28, 28) stitches. Work in stockinette stitch for 5 (5½, 6) inches (12.5, 13.8, 15 cm), ending with a purl row. Next row, *knit 2, knit 2 together, repeat from * across row. Purl 1 row. Next row, *knit 1, knit 2 together, repeat from * across row. Purl 1 row. Next row, knit 2 together across row. Break yarn, leaving a long end. Pull this end through remaining stitches and, with same yarn, sew about 1 inch (2.5 cm) from Back.

Finishing
Join yarn at back of Hat. Work 1 row single crochet along bottom edge. Chain 30 for tie. Work single crochet on these 30 stitches, continue in single crochet along front edge of Hat. Make another tie. Continue to back, where you joined, do not break yarn. Work 1 row single crochet backwards over all stitches, omitting ties. Do not steam.

Young Man's Wishbone Cable Pullover

See photograph C-1 in color section.

Young Men's Sizes

Directions are for size 12. Changes for sizes 14 and 16 are in parentheses.

Materials

10 (11, 12) skeins (4 oz or 112 g each) Bulky by Spinnerin or any bulky yarn to give gauge

Needles

#15
#17
double-pointed cable needle
2 stitch holders

Gauge

2 stitches = 1 inch (2.5 cm)

Note: Yarn is used double strand throughout.

Pattern

Row 1 (right side):
Purl 4 (5, 6), knit 4, purl 4, knit 8, purl 4, knit 4, purl 4 (5, 6).
Row 2: Knit 4 (5, 6), purl 4, knit 4, knit 8, knit 4, purl 4, knit 4 (5, 6).
Row 3: Purl 4 (5, 6), *slip next 2 stitches onto double-pointed cable needle, hold to back, knit next 2 stitches, knit 2 from needle, *purl 4, knit 8, purl 4, repeat between *s once, purl 4 (5, 6).
Row 4: Work same as Row 2.
Row 5: Work same as Row 3.
Row 6: Work same as Row 2.
Row 7: Work same as Row 3.
Row 8: Work same as Row 2.
Row 9: Purl 4 (5, 6), repeat between *s of Row 3 once, purl 4, slip next 2 stitches to double-pointed needle, hold to back, knit next 2 stitches, knit 2 from double-pointed needle, slip next 2 stitches to double-pointed needle, hold to front, knit next 2 stitches, knit 2 from double-pointed needle, purl 4, repeat between *s of Row 3 once, purl 4 (5, 6).

Back

With #15 needles, cast on 32 (34, 36) stitches. Work in knit 1, purl 1 ribbing for 3 (7.5 cm) inches. Change to #17 needles and work in pattern until 12 (13, 14) inches (30, 32.5, 35 cm) from beginning. At the beginning of the next 2 rows, bind off 2 stitches. Work even until armhole measures 7 (7½, 8) inches (17.5, 18.8, 20 cm). At the beginning of the next 2 rows, bind off 6 (7, 7) stitches. Place remaining stitches on stitch holder.

Front

Work same as Back until armhole measures 5½ (6, 6) inches (13.8, 15, 15 cm). Work across 8 (9, 9) stitches. Place center 12 (12, 14) stitches on a stitch holder. Join new yarn. Work remaining 8 (9, 9) stitches. Continue in pattern, decreasing 1 stitch at neck edge every row, 2 times, bind off remaining stitches.

Neckband

Sew shoulders together on 1 side. With right side of garment facing you, use #15 needle to pick up 38 (38, 40) stitches around neck, including stitches on holders. Work in knit 1, purl 1 ribbing for 3 inches (7.5 cm). Change to #17 needles. Continue ribbing until collar measures 4½ inches (11.3 cm), bind off loosely in ribbing pattern. Sew other shoulder.

Sleeves

With right side facing you, pick up 24 (26, 26) stitches along armhole.
Row 1 (wrong side): Knit 6 (7, 7), purl 4, knit 4, purl 4, knit 6 (7, 7).
Row 2: Purl 6 (7, 7) *slip next 2 stitches onto double-pointed needle, hold to back, knit 2, knit 2 from double-pointed needle, * purl 4, repeat between *s once, purl 6 (7, 7).
Repeat Rows 1 and 2. Work even for 8 inches (20 cm), decreasing 1 stitch each side, once. Work even for 5 inches (12.5 cm), decreasing 1 stitch each side, once. Work even for 0 (1, 2) inches. Change to #15 needles, and work in knit 1, purl 1 ribbing for 3 inches (7.5 cm), bind off in ribbing pattern.

Finishing

Sew underarm seams. Do not block.

Woman's Garter-Stitch Pullover

See photograph C-2 in color section.

Women's Sizes
Directions are for small size. Changes for medium and large sizes are in parentheses.

Materials
4 (5, 5) skeins (2 oz or 56 g each) Mirabella by Stanley Berocco or any mohair yarn to give gauge

4 (5, 5) skeins (2 oz or 56 g each) Dji Dji by Stanley Berocco or any mohair yarn to give gauge

Needles
#15
#17

Gauge
2 stitches = 1 inch (2.5 cm)

Note: Yarn is used one strand of each held together throughout garment.

Back
With #15 needles, cast on 36 (38, 40) stitches. Work in knit 1, purl 1 ribbing for 8 inches (20 cm). Change to #17 needles. Work garter stitch (knit every row) till 25 (25½, 26) inches (62.5, 63.8, 65 cm) from beginning. Bind off all stitches.

Front
Work same as Back. Sew 1 shoulder 5 (5½, 6) inches (12.5, 13.8, 15 cm) in from outside edge. With #15 needles, right side facing you, and starting 5 (5½, 6) inches from other side, pick up 40 (42, 44) stitches around neck edge. Knit 1, purl 1, in ribbing for 2 inches (5 cm), change to #17 needles. Continue ribbing till 8 inches (20 cm) from beginning, bind off in ribbing. Sew other shoulder and turtle neck.

Sleeves
Allowing 8 (8½, 8½) inches (20, 21.3, 21.3 cm) from shoulder for armhole, pick up 26 (28, 30) stitches along armhole. Work even for 15 (16, 17) inches (37.5, 40, 42.5 cm), change to #15 needles. Work knit 1, purl 1 ribbing for 8 inches (20 cm), bind off in ribbing.

Finishing
Sew underarm seams. Do not block.

Man's Striped, Textured Pullover

See photograph C-3 in color section.

Men's Sizes
Directions are for small size. Changes for medium and large sizes are in parentheses.

Materials
4 (5, 5) skeins (3½ oz or 110 g each) Vail Homespun by Brunswick in Color A or any bulky yarn to give gauge
3 skeins in Color B
3 skeins in Color C

Needles
#15
#17

Gauge
2 stitches = 1 inch (2.5 cm)

Pattern
Row 1 (right side): With Color B, knit 4, *slip 1, knit 3, repeat from * to last stitch, knit 1.
Row 2: With Color B, purl 4, *slip 1, purl 3, repeat from * across row to last stitch, purl 1.
Rows 3-4: With Color B, knit across.
Row 5: With Color A, knit 2, *slip 1, knit 3, repeat from * to last 3 stitches, slip 1, knit 2.
Row 6: With Color A, purl 2, *slip 1, purl 3, repeat from * to last 3 stitches, slip 1, purl 2.
Rows 7-8: With Color A, knit across.
Rows 9-12: Join Color C, repeat Rows 1-4.
Rows 13-16: Join Color A, repeat Rows 5-8.

Back
With #15 needles and Color A, cast on 36 (40, 44) stitches. Knit 1, purl 1 in ribbing for 3 inches (7.5 cm), increasing 1 stitch at end of last row. Change to #17 needles and work till 24 (25, 26) inches (60, 62.5, 65 cm), from beginning. Work across 13 (14, 15) stitches, place center 11 (13, 15) stitches on holder, join new yarn, work remaining 13 (14, 15) stitches. Working both sides at once, decreasing 1 stitch at neck edge every row, 2 times, bind off remaining 11 (12, 13) stitches each side.

Front
Work same as Back till 22 (23, 24) inches (55, 57.5, 60 cm) from beginning. Shape neck as Back, work even to shoulder, then bind off remaining 11 (12, 13) stitches each side. Sew 1 shoulder seam, leaving bound-off stitches to outside to form saddle shoulder.

Neckband
With Color A, #15 needles, and right side facing you, pick up 40 (42, 44) stitches around neck edge, including stitches on holders. Knit 1, purl 1 in ribbing for 1 inch (2.5 cm), bind off in ribbing. Sew other shoulder.

Sleeves
With Color A, #17 needles, and right side facing you, allowing 9 inches each side of shoulder seam for sleeve, pick up 28 (30, 32) stitches along armhole edge. Continuing with Color A, starting with Row 6 of pattern, work for 4 inches (10 cm), then decrease 1 stitch each side. Being careful to keep pattern as established, continue to decrease 1 stitch each side every 4 inches (10 cm), 2 times more. Work even till sleeve is 18 (19, 20) inches (45, 47.5, 50 cm). Changes to #15 needles and Color A. Knit 1, purl 1 in ribbing for 3 inches (7.5 cm), bind off in ribbing.

Finishing
Sew underarm seams. Block by steaming gently with a pressing cloth, wrong side out.

Woman's Mohair Cable Cardigan

See photograph C-4 in color section.

Women's Sizes
Directions are for small size. Changes for medium and large sizes are in parentheses.

Materials
12 (12, 13) skeins (1½ oz or 40 g each) Majestic Mohair by Galler or any mohair yarn to give gauge

Needles
#13
#15
#10½ crochet hook

Gauge
2 stitches = 1 inch (2.5 cm)

Pattern
Row 1 (wrong side): Knit 7 (8, 9), *purl 2, knit 5, repeat from * ending with knit 7 (8, 9).
Row 2: Purl 7 (8, 9), *knit 1, yarn over, knit 1, purl 5, repeat from * ending with purl 7 (8, 9).
Row 3: Knit 7 (8, 9), *purl 3, knit 5, repeat from * ending with knit 7 (8, 9).
Row 4: Purl 7 (8, 9), *slip 1, knit 2, pass the slipped stitch over both knit stitches, purl 5, repeat from * ending with purl 7 (8, 9).
Row 5: Knit 7 (8, 9), *purl 2, knit 5, repeat from * ending with knit 7 (8, 9).

Back
With #13 needles, cast on 36 (38, 40) stitches. Knit 1, purl 1 in ribbing for 3 inches (7.5 cm). Add 1 stitch at end of last row. Change to #15 needles and work pattern till 16 (17, 18) inches (40, 42.5, 45 cm) or desired length to underarm. At the beginning of the next 2 rows, bind off 3 stitches. Then decrease 1 stitch each side, every other row, 3 (4, 4) times. Work even till armhole is 7½ (8, 8½) inches (18.8, 20, 21.3 cm). At the beginning of the next 2 rows, bind off 8 stitches. Bind off remaining stitches.

Left Front
Cast on 23 (24, 25) stitches. Knit 1, purl 1 in ribbing for 3 inches (7.5 cm). Change to #15 needles and work pattern as on Back. Work till armhole, shape arm side as Back. Work even till 6½ (7, 7½) inches (16.3, 17.5, 18.8 cm), ending at front edge. Bind off 7 stitches at front edge. Decrease 1 stitch front edge 2 times. Work even till shoulder, bind off remaining stitches.

Right Front
Work same as Left Front, reversing all shaping.

Sleeves
With #13 needles, cast on 20 stitches. Knit 1, purl 1 in ribbing for 3 inches (7.5 cm). Change to #15 needles. Knit 1 row, increasing evenly spaced to 23 (25, 27) stitches. Work pattern as on Back till 6 inches (15 cm) from beginning. Increase 1 stitch each side and repeat this increase after 4 inches (10 cm). Work even till 16 (17, 18) inches (40, 42.5, 45 cm) from beginning. At the beginning of the next 2 rows, bind off 3 stitches. Decrease 1 stitch each side, every other row, till 9 stitches remain, bind off. Sew shoulder seams. With #13 needles and right side facing you, pick up 33 (33, 35) stitches along neck edge. Knit 1, purl 1 in ribbing for 3 inches (7.5 cm), bind off in ribbing.

Finishing
Set in sleeves, sew underarm seams. Starting at bottom right front, work 1 row single crochet along front edge, making 6 buttonholes evenly spaced, chain 1 turn, make a 2nd row of single crochet, making 2 stitches in each buttonhole. Starting at left top front, work 2 rows single crochet along left front. Do not block. To make buttonholes: chain 2, skip 1.

Woman's Mohair Cable Pullover

See photograph C-5 in color section.

Women's Sizes
Directions are for small size. Changes for medium and large sizes are in parentheses.

Materials
12 (12, 13) skeins (1½ oz or 40 g each) Majestic Mohair by Galler or any mohair yarn to give gauge

Needles
#13
#15
#10½ crochet hook

Gauge
2 stitches = 1 inch (2.5 cm)

Note: Yarn is used double strand throughout.

Pattern
Row 1 (wrong side): Knit 7 (8, 9) *purl 2, knit 5, repeat from * ending with knit 7 (8, 9).
Row 2: Purl 7 (8, 9), *knit 1, yarn over, knit 1, purl 5, repeat from * ending with purl 7 (8, 9).
Row 3: Knit 7 (8, 9), *purl 3, knit 5, repeat from * ending with knit 7 (8, 9).
Row 4: Purl 7 (8, 9), *slip 1, knit 2, pass the slipped stitch over both knit stitches, purl 5, repeat from * ending with purl 7 (8, 9).
Row 5: Knit 7 (8, 9), *purl 2, knit 5, repeat from * ending with knit 7 (8, 9).

Back
With #13 needles, cast on 36 (38, 40) stitches. Knit 1, purl 1 in ribbing for 3 inches (7.5 cm). Add 1 stitch at end of last row. Change to #15 needles and work pattern till 16 (17, 18) inches (40, 42.5, 45 cm) or desired length to underarm. At the beginning of the next 2 rows, bind off 3 stitches. Then decrease 1 stitch each side, every other row, 3 (4, 4) times. Work even till armhole is 7½ (8, 8½) inches (18.8, 20, 21.3 cm). At the beginning of the next 2 rows, bind off 8 stitches. Place remaining stitches on holder.

Front
Work same as Back till armhole is 5½ (6, 6½) inches (13.8, 15, 16.3 cm), then shape neck as follows: Work across 10 stitches, place center 5 (5, 7) stitches on holder, join new yarn, and work remaining 10 stitches. Continuing in pattern, working each side with separate ball of yarn, decrease 1 stitch each neck edge, every row, 2 times. Work even on remaining 8 stitches to shoulder, bind off.

Sleeves
With #13 needles, cast on 20 stitches. Knit 1, purl 1 in ribbing for 3 inches (7.5 cm). Change to #15 needles. Knit 1 row, increasing evenly spaced to 23 (25, 27) stitches. Work pattern as on Back till 6 inches (15 cm) from beginning. Increase 1 stitch each side and repeat this increase after 4 inches (10 cm) more are worked. Work even till 16 (17, 18) inches (40, 42.5, 45 cm) or desired length. At the beginning of the next 2 rows, bind off 3 stitches. Decrease 1 stitch each side every other row till 9 stitches remain, bind off. Sew 1 shoulder seam. With right side facing you, pick up 33 (33, 35) stitches around neck, including those on holders. Knit 1, purl 1 in ribbing for 2 inches (5 cm), bind off loosely. Sew other shoulder, including neckband.

Finishing
Sew underarm seams. Set in sleeves. Do not block.

Woman's Tweed Tunic

See photograph C-6 in color section.

Women's Sizes
Directions are for small size. Changes for medium and large sizes are in parentheses.

Materials
18 (20, 22) skeins (7/10 oz or 46 g each) Knob Tweed by Unger or any bulky yarn to give gauge

Needles
#19
#10½ crochet hook

Gauge
1½ stitches = 1 inch (2.5 cm)

Note: Yarn is used double strand throughout.

Pattern for Bottom, Sleeves, Yoke, and Collar
Row 1: Knit across row.
Row 2: *Knit 1, purl 1, repeat from * across row.

Back
With #19 needles, cast on 28 (30, 32) stitches. Work pattern for 6 rows, then work in stockinette stitch (knit 1 row, purl 1 row) till 15½ (16, 16½) inches (38.8, 40, 41.3 cm) from beginning. At the beginning of the next 2 rows, bind off 2 stitches. Now work in pattern till yoke is 7 (7½, 8) inches (17.5, 18.8, 20 cm). At the beginning of the next 2 rows, bind off 8 (8, 9) stitches. Bind off remaining 8 (10, 10) stitches.

Front
Work same as Back till armhole stitches are bound off. Work in pattern for Yoke. Work across next 10 (11, 12) stitches, join new yarn, bind off center 4 stitches, work remaining 10 (11, 12) stitches. Continuing in pattern and working each side with separate yarn, decrease 1 stitch each next edge, every 4th row, 2 (3, 3) times. Work even in pattern to shoulder, bind off remaining 8 (8, 9) stitches left each side. Sew shoulder seams, leaving bound-off edge to outside to form saddle shoulder.

Sleeves
With right side facing you, pick up 20 (22, 24) stitches along armhole. Work in pattern for 12 (13, 14) inches (30, 32.5, 35 cm). Reverse pattern, work 4 inches (10 cm) more, bind off.

Collar
With right side facing you and #19 needles, pick up 34 (36, 38) stitches around neck edge. Work in pattern stitch (right side of pattern should be facing wrong side of sweater) for 4 inches (10 cm), bind off. Work 1 row of single crochet around neck opening and collar, making a buttonloop (chain 6, make a single crochet in same stitch) at right neck edge. Sew underarm seams. Do not block.

Finishing
Sew underarm seams. Do not block.

Woman's Super-Easy Pullover

See photograph C-7 in color section.

Women's Sizes

Directions are for small size. Changes for medium and large sizes are in parentheses.

Materials

6 (7, 7) skeins (3½ oz or 100 g each) Super Heavy Donegal Tweed by Tahki or any bulky tweed yarn to give gauge

6 (7, 7) skeins (2 oz or 56 g each) Michelaine by Tahki or any bulky yarn to give gauge

Needles

#17

Gauge

2 stitches = 1 inch (2.5 cm)

Note: Use one strand of each yarn held together throughout.

Back

With #17 needles, cast on 35 (37, 39) stitches. Knit 1, purl 1 in ribbing for 13 (13½, 14) inches (32.5, 33.8, 40 cm). Mark for armholes, continue ribbing for 7 (7½, 8) inches (17.5, 18.8, 20 cm) more, bind off.

Front

Work same as Back.

Sleeves

Sew shoulder seam by weaving 5½ (6, 6) inches (13.8, 15, 15 cm) in from each side. Pick up 22 (24, 26) stitches from marker to marker, leaving 11 (12, 13) stitches on each side of shoulder seam. Knit 1, purl 1 in ribbing for 22 (23, 24) inches (55, 57.5, 60 cm), bind off.

Finishing

Sew underarm seams and fold back cuff.

Woman's Multi-Yarn Cardigan

See photograph C-8 in color section.

Woman's Sizes
Directions are for small size. Changes for medium and large sizes are in parentheses.

Materials
3 skeins (3½ oz or 100 g each) Germantown Knitting Worsted by Brunswick or any knitting worsted to give gauge

3 skeins (1½ oz or 40 g each) Majestic Mohair by Galler or any mohair to give gauge

3 skeins (1¾ oz or 50 g each) Nubs and Slubs by Stanley Berocco

3 skeins (2 oz or 56 g each) Dji Dji by Stanley Berocco

5 skeins (2 oz or 56 g each) **Zoom** Zoom by Stanley Berocco

Close-up view of stitching on Woman's Multi-Yarn Cardigan. See photograph C-8 in color section.

Needles
#13
#15
#10½ crochet hook

Gauge
2 stitches = 1 inch (2.5 cm)

Back
With a double strand of knitting worsted and #13 needles, cast on 42 (44, 46) stitches. Knit 1, purl 1 in ribbing for 3 inches (7.5 cm). On next row, break worsted, join 1 strand mohair and 1 strand Nubs and Slubs, and, using #15 needles, knit 1 row, knit another row, purl 1 row, (purl side is right side). Continue in reverse stockinette stitch for 5½ inches (13.8 cm), break yarn, join double strand of knitting worsted, and knit 4 rows. Break worsted, join single strand of Zoom Zoom and work another stripe in reverse stockinette stitch for 5½ inches (13.8 cm). Break yarn, join double strand of worsted and knit 4 rows. Break worsted, join a double strand of Dji Dji and work as follows (this will begin raglan shaping): (Wrong side) Purl 3 stitches, * knit 1, purl 1 in ribbing to last 3 stitches, purl 3. Next row, knit 3, knit 2 together, follow stitches to last 5 stitches, knit 2 together, knit last 3 stitches. Next row, purl 3, reverse stitches (knit over purl stitches, and purl over knit stitches) to last 3, purl 3. Next row, knit 3, knit 2 together, follow stitches to last 5 stitches, knit 2 together, knit last 3. Repeat the last 4 rows till raglan is 10½ (11, 11½) inches (26.3, 27.5, 28.3 cm). Bind off remaining stitches. (See photograph for close-up view.)

48

C-1

C-3

C-2

C-4

C-5

C-7

C-6

C-8

C-9

C-1 (See directions on page 40.)
Young Man's Wishbone Cable Pullover
When knitted on large needles, the simple wishbone cable gives a very dramatic look. This effect is achieved with a minimum of effort.

C-2 (See directions on page 42.)
Women's Garter-Stitch Pullover
One of the easiest patterns in the book, this lovely sweater is a combination of ribbing and garter stitch. It's great for outdoor activity.

C-3 (See directions on page 43.)
Man's Striped, Textured Pullover
This unusual striped sweater is easier than it looks. We used a three-color pattern for this handsome sweater. The adventuresome might make each stripe a different color.

C-4 (See directions on page 44.)
Woman's Mohair Cable Cardigan
Cables magnified by the jumbo needles look super. The soft mohair yarn makes a luxuriously soft sweater.

C-5 (See directions on page 45.)
Woman's Mohair Cable Pullover
Both the cardigan and pullover versions of this sweater are easy to do, and the results are rewarding.

C-6 (See directions on page 46.)
Woman's Tweed Tunic
The simple technique of using reverse sides of the same pattern was used to create the yoked look in this sweater.

C-7 (See directions on page 47.)
Woman's Super-Easy Pullover
This really is a super easy sweater and it is perfect for a first project. It is done with one simple stitch, and there are no increases or decreases in the pattern.

C-8 (See directions on page 48.)
Woman's Multi-Yarn Cardigan
A combination of 5 different yarns were used to create the unique look of this sweater. Use the same yarns we did or mix and match your own. Just be sure that the yarns give the same gauge as ours.

C-9 (See directions on page 50.)
Quick-Knit Pillows
Pillows are great fun to make—they are easy and very rewarding to complete. Designer looks can be achieved with just a bit of imagination and the use of different yarn combinations. Shown in the picture are Sand-Stitch Floor Pillow (top left), Honeycomb Pillow (top right), Homespun Throw Pillow (bottom left), and Garter-Stitch Throw Pillow (bottom right).

C-10

C-12

C-11

C-10 (See directions on pages 54 and 55.)
Woman's Bulky Pullover With Stripes and Woman's Textured Vest
The striping pattern on this classic white pullover is still another example of the interesting effects that small variations can produce in a finished garment. On the other hand, it's the heavily textured yarn that adds excitement to this simple vest. Contrasting borders set off the multicolored yarn.

C-11 (See directions on page 56.)
Woman's Mohair Coat
This coat was done in two shades of pink for a subtle tweed effect. It was knitted in separate panels, then joined together at the yoke.

C-12 (See directions on page 57.)
Woman's Mohair Coat, Hat, and Scarf Set
The hat and scarf complete the look of this coat ensemble.

Front

Cast on 21 (22, 23) stitches. Work same as Back till start of raglan shaping. Then shape arm sides as back, keeping front edges even. Work till raglan is 8 (8½, 9) inches (20, 21.3, 22.5 cm), ending at front edge. Bind off 6 stitches at front edge, continue raglan shaping as established, and, at the same time, decrease 1 stitch neck edge, every other row. Work in this manner till 2 stitches remain, bind off.

Sleeves

With #13 needles, cast on 22 (24, 26) stitches. Using double strand of worsted, knit 1, purl 1 in ribbing for 3 inches (7.5 cm). On the next row, knit across row increasing evenly to 28 (30, 32) stitches. Work same as Back, bind off remaining stitches.

Finishing

Sew all seams. With right side facing you, using double strand of worsted and the #13 needle, pick up 49 (51, 53) stitches along neck edge. (An odd number of stitches are picked up so that each side of the collar will begin and end with a knit stitch. Be sure to keep rib pattern when working.) Work in knit 1, purl 1 ribbing for 4 inches (10 cm). Change to #15 needles and continue ribbing for 4 inches (10 cm) more, bind off in ribbing. Starting at bottom righthand corner, using double strand of worsted yarn, work 1 row single crochet along front edge, right to edge of collar, chain 1, turn. Work a second row of single crochet, chain 1, turn. On the third row of single crochet, work buttonholes as follows: chain 2, skip 2 stitches, make a buttonhole 1 inch (2.5 cm) from bottom, make a buttonhole at each worsted stripe, make fourth buttonhole at start of collar. Work 2 more rows of single crochet, making 2 single crochet in each buttonhole space, do not break yarn and do not turn. Work 1 row backward single crochet along front edge, end off. Work other side to correspond, making 1 buttonhole at base of collar on left side. End off. Do not block.

Quick-Knit Pillows

Pillows are fun to make and easy too. By using almost any bulky yarn double strand and #17 knitting needles, you can establish a gauge of 2 stitches to the inch. Just measure your pillow, multiply by 2, and cast on that number of stitches. Then knit away in any pattern till your desired length and bind off. Make another piece the same size and then crochet or sew together 3 sides, stuff your pillow, and sew the remaining side. You now have a gorgeous pillow, to which you can fringe or tassels if you like. The four pillows shown in photograph C-9 in the color section are made in this manner. The instructions follow.

Sand-Stitch Floor Pillow

Size
36 inches square

Materials
8 skeins (3½ oz or 100 g each) knitting worsted
uncovered pillow form, 36 by 36 inches (90 by
  90 cm)
1 yard of 36-inch-wide (90-cm) fabric

Needles
#17

Gauge
2 stitches = 1 inch (2.5 cm)

Note: The knitting worsted was used 4 strand
to give the same effect as 2 strands of bulky
yarn.

Pattern
Row 1: Knit across row.
Row 2: Knit 1, purl 1 in rib across row.
With #17 needles, cast on 72 stitches. Work
pattern for 36 inches (90 cm), bind off. Fringe
all around if desired. (See photograph for close-
up view.)

Pillow
With #17 needles, cast on 72 stitches. Work
pattern for 36 inches (90 cm), bind off.

Finishing
Fringe all around if desired. (See photograph
for close-up view.)

Close-up view of Sand-Stitch Floor Pillow stitching
pattern. See photograph C-9 in color section.

Honeycomb Pillow

Size
24 inches square

Materials
8 skeins (3½ oz or 100 g each) of knitting-worsted
uncovered pillow form, 24 by 24 inches (60 by 60 cm)

Needles
#17
1 bulky cable needle

Gauge
2 stitches = 1 inch (2.5 cm)

Note: This pattern is a little more difficult, but makes a very interesting pillow. Again, 4 strands of knitting worsted were used to give the same effect as 2 strands of bulky yarn.

Pattern
Row 1 (wrong side): Knit 2, purl 6, knit 2, purl 32, knit 2, purl 6, knit 2.
Row 2: Purl 2, knit 6, purl 2, knit 32, purl 2, knit 6, purl 2.
Row 3: Work same as Row 1.
Row 4: Purl 2, slip next 3 stitches to a double-pointed needle, hold to back of work, knit next 3 stitches, knit 3 from double-pointed needle, purl 2, *slip next 2 stitches to double-pointed needle, hold to back of work, knit next 2 stitches, knit the 2 from double-pointed needle, slip next 2 stitches to double-pointed needle, hold to front of work, knit next 2 stitches, knit the 2 from the double-pointed needle, repeat from * 3 times more, purl 2, slip next 3 stitches to double-pointed needle, hold to back of work, knit next 3 stitches, knit 3 from double-pointed needle, purl 2.
Row 5: Work same as Row 1.
Row 6: Work same as Row 2.
Row 7: Work same as Row 1.
Row 8: Purl 2, knit 6, purl 2, *slip 2 stitches to double-pointed needle, hold to front of work, knit next 2 stitches, knit 2 from double-pointed needle. Slip next 2 stitches to double-pointed needle, hold to back of work, knit next 2, knit 2 from double-pointed needle, repeat from * 3 times more, purl 2, knit 6, purl 2.
Row 9: Work same as Row 1.
Row 10: Work same as Row 2.
Row 11: Work same as Row 1.
Row 12: Work same as Row 4.

Pillow
Repeat the last 12 rows till pillow is 24 inches (60 cm) long, bind off. Repeat for 2nd piece.

Finishing
Holding both pieces, wrong sides together, work 1 row single crochet between both thicknesses. Work around 3 sides. Put pillow form inside and continue working last side. Join, do not break yarn. Work 1 row single crochet backwards around entire outside edge. Make 4 large tassels, placing 1 in each corner.

Homespun Throw Pillow

Size
14 inches square

Materials
1 skein (2 oz or 56 g each) Aspen by Brunswick
or any bulky yarn to give gauge
1 skein (3½ oz or 100 g each) Vail Homespun by
Brunswick or any bulky yarn to give gauge
1 skein (3½ oz or 100 g each) Columbian Handspun by Tahki (a very nubby yarn) or any
textured yarn to give gauge
uncovered pillow form, 14 by 14 inches (35 by
35 cm)

Needles
#14

Gauge
2 stitches = 1 inch (2.5 cm)

Pillow
Using a double strand of Vail, cast on 24
stitches. Work in reverse stockinette stitch
throughout as follows:
Rows 1-4: Double strand of Vail.
Rows 5-10: Change to Aspen.
Rows 11-16: Change to Columbian Handspun.
Rows 17-19: Change to Aspen.
Rows 20-25: Change to Columbia Handspun.
Rows 26-29: Change to Aspen.
Rows 30-33: Change to Vail.
Bind off, make the 2nd piece and sew or crochet
together around three sides. Stuff and sew up
the third side.

Finishing
This pillow is pretty just as is, but add fringe if
you like.

Garter-Stitch Throw Pillow

Size
14 inches square

Materials
3 skeins (2 oz or 56 g each) Aspen by Brunswick
or any bulky yarn to give gauge
small amount in contrasting color
uncovered pillow form, 14 by 14 inches (35 by
35 cm)

Needles
#17

Gauge
2 stitches = 1 inch (2.5 cm)

Note: Yarn is used double strand throughout.
Garter stitch stretches, so make a 12-inch (30-
cm) pillow and stretch it to 14 inches (35 cm).

Pillow
Cast on 24 stitches. Knit every row for 12 inches
(30 cm), bind off. Make a 2nd piece. Sew or crochet edges together. Using 2 strands of a contrasting color, weave in and out of stitches at
center. Weave a 2nd and 3rd row in either side
of the center row.

Finishing
Using the contrasting color make a pom pom
and attach in center. Fringe all around for a
plush look.

Woman's Bulky Pullover With Stripes

See photograph C-10 in color section.

Women's Sizes
Directions are for small size. Changes for medium and large sizes are in parentheses.

Materials
10 skeins (2 oz or 56 g each) Aspen by Brunswick yarn in Color A or any bulky yarn to give gauge
2 skeins in Color B

Needles
#15
#17

Gauge
2 stitches = 1 inch (2.5 cm)

Note: Yarn is used double strand throughout.

Back
With #15 needles and Color B, cast on 34 (36, 38) stitches. Work in knit 1, purl 1 ribbing for 5 rows, drop Color B. Using 2 strands of Color A, continue ribbing for 4 more rows. Using 1 strand of Color A and 1 strand of Color B, continue ribbing for 4 more rows. Changing to #17 needles and 2 strands of Color A, continue in stockinette stitch (knit 1 row, purl 1 row) till 16 (16½, 17) inches (40, 41.3, 42.5 cm) or desired length to underarm. Mark each side for armholes. Continue in stockinette stitch till 6 (6½, 7) inches (15, 16.3, 17.5 cm) above marker. Work across 13 stitches, place center 8 (10, 12) stitches on a holder, join new yarn, work remaining 13 stitches. Continue in stockinette stitch, decreasing 1 stitch each neck edge, every row, 3 times. Bind off remaining 10 stitches.

Front
Work same as Back till 5 (5½, 6) inches (12.5, 13.8, 15 cm) above armhole marker. Shape neck as Back, work even till shoulder, bind off.

Neckband
Sew one shoulder seam, leaving bound-off stitches to outside to form saddle shoulder. With #15 needles, Color A and with right side facing you, pick up 40 (42, 44) stitches around neck edge, including stitches on holders. Knit 1, purl 1 in ribbing for 4 rows, bind off in ribbing. Sew other shoulder seam.

Sleeves
Using #17 needles and one strand of Color A with 1 strand Color B, and with right side facing you, pick up 24 (26, 28) stitches from armhole marker to armhole marker. Work 4 rows, knit 1, purl 1 ribbing, then continue with Color A in stockinette stitch for 4 inches (10 cm). Decrease 1 stitch each side and repeat the decrease every 4 inches 1 (2, 2) time more. Work even till 14 (15, 16) inches (35, 37.5, 40 cm). Change to #15 needles. Knit 1, purl 1 in ribbing for 5 inches (12.5 cm), bind off in ribbing.

Finishing
Sew underarm seams. Block gently with pressing cloth, wrong side out.

54

Woman's Textured Vest

See photograph C-10 in color section.

Women's Sizes
Directions are for small size. Changes for medium and large sizes are in parentheses.

Materials
8 (9, 9) skeins (2 oz or 56 g each) Bim Bam by Stanley Berocco or any textured yarn to give gauge

2 skeins (3½ oz or 100 g each) knitting worsted

Needles
#11
#15
#10½ crochet hook

Gauge
2 stitches = 1 inch (2.5 cm)

Note: Yarn is used double strand throughout.

Back
With #11 needles and knitting worsted, cast on 32 (34, 36) stitches. Work in ribbing of knit 1, purl 1 for 3 inches (7.5 cm). Change to Bim Bam and work in stockinette stitch (knit 1 row, purl 1 row) till 10 (11, 12) inches (25, 27.5, 30 cm) from beginning or desired length to underarm. At the beginning of the next 2 rows, bind off 2 stitches. Then decrease 1 stitch each side, every other row, 2 times. Work even in stockinette stitch till armhole is 8 (8½, 9) inches (20, 21.3, 22.5 cm). At the beginning of the next 2 rows, bind off 6 stitches. Bind off remaining stitches.

Right Front
Cast on 16 (17, 18) stitches. Work same as Back to armhole. Shape arm side same as Back, keeping front edges even. Work till armhole is 5 (5½, 6) inches (12.5, 13.8, 15 cm), ending at front edge. Bind off 3 (4, 5) stitches, finish row. Continuing in stockinette stitch, decrease 1 stitch neck edge, every row, 3 times. Work even to shoulder, bind off remaining 6 stitches.

Left Front
Work same as Right Front, reversing all shaping.

Finishing
Using purl side as outside, sew shoulder seams, sew side seams. Work 1 row single crochet around front, neck, and armhole edges. Do not block.

Woman's Mohair Coat, Hat, and Scarf Set

See photographs C-11 and C-12 in color section.

Coat

Women's Sizes
Fits all sizes between 6 and 14.

Materials
8 skeins (2 oz or 56 g each) Mirabella by Stanley Berocco in Color A or any mohair to give gauge
8 skeins in Color B
hooks and eyes (optional)

Needles
#17
#15 circular
#10½ crochet hook
4 large stitch holders

Gauge
5 stitches = 3 inches (7.5 cm)
2 rows = 1 inch

Note: Yarn is worked 1 strand of each yarn held together. All panels begin and end with garter-stitch band. Directions are for 36-inch (90-cm) length from hem to underarm. To shorten or lengthen coat add or subtract rows from the stockinette-stitch bands.

Back
With #17 needles, cast on 48 stitches. The piece should measure 28 stitches across. Work pattern of 9 rows garter stitch (knit each row), 8 rows stockinette stitch (knit 1 row, purl 1 row). Work even, repeating pattern until there are 5 sets of garter-stitch bands and 4 sets of stockinette-stitch bands. Place panel on stitch holder.

Left Front
Cast on 26 stitches and work same pattern as Back. Place panel on stitch holder.

Right Front
Cast on and work same as Left Front. Place panel on stitch holder.

Sleeves
Cast on 24 stitches and work in pattern until there are 3 sets of garter-stitch bands and 2 sets of stockinette-stitch bands. Place sleeve panels on stitch holders.

Yoke
With #15 circular needle, pick up all panels as follows: Right Front, Sleeve, Back, Sleeve, and Left Front.
Row 1 (right side): Knit, decreasing 16 stitches evenly spaced across row.
Row 2: Purl.
Row 3: Knit, decreasing 16 stitches evenly spaced across row.
Rows 4-12: Work in garter stitch.
Row 13: Knit, decreasing 16 stitches evenly spaced across row.
Row 14: Purl.
Row 15: Knit, decreasing 16 stitches evenly spaced across row.
Rows 16-24: Work in garter stitch.
Row 25: Knit, decreasing 16 stitches evenly spaced across row.
Row 26: Purl.
Row 27: Knit, decreasing 16 stitches evenly spaced across row.
Rows 28-36: Work in garter stitch.
Row 37: Knit, decreasing 16 stitches evenly spaced across row.
Row 38: Purl.
Row 39: Knit, decreasing 16 stitches evenly spaced across row.

Bow Tie

Cast on 50 stitches at the beginning of the next 2 rows. Work 9 rows of garter stitch, bind off loosely.

Finishing

Sew seam from wrist to halfway down side seam. Sew a narrow hem at the wrists and insert elastic band. Starting at left neck edge, work 1 row of single crochet around entire outside edge of garment, making 3 single crochets in each corner to turn. Sew hooks along front of yoke, if desired.

Hat

Sizes
One size fits all.

Materials
1 skein (2 oz or 56 g each) Mirabella by Stanley Berocco in Color A or any mohair yarn to give gauge
1 skein in Color B

Needles
#17

Gauge
2 stitches = 1 inch (2.5 cm)

Note: Yarn is worked 1 strand of each color held together throughout.

Hat
With #17 needles, cast on 36 stitches. Work every row in garter stitch (knit each row) for 12 inches (30 cm). On next row, knit 2 together across row. On next row, knit 2 together across row again, do not bind off. Cut yarn, leaving a long end. Pull this end through remaining stitches. With same yarn weave seam.

Finishing
Roll cuff in a tight roll, stitch in place. Do not block.

Scarf

Sizes
One size fits all.

Materials
2 skeins (2 oz or 56 g each) Mirabella by Stanley Berocco in Color A or any mohair yarn to give gauge
2 skeins in Color B

Needles
#17

Gauge
2 stitches = 1 inch (2.5 cm)

Note: Yarn is used 1 strand of each held together throughout.

Scarf
With #17 needles, cast on 18 stitches. Work every row in garter stitch (knit each row) for 72 inches (180 cm). Bind off. Cut yarn in 12-inch (30-cm) lengths and fringe.

Finishing
Do not block.

Two-Toned Hat and Scarf Set

Sizes
One size fits all.

Materials
3 skeins (2 oz or 56 g each) Bulky Nantuck by
  Columbia Minerva in Color A or any bulky
  yarn to give gauge
3 skeins in Color B

Needles
#17
#10½ crochet hook

Gauge
2 stitches = 1 inch (2.5 cm)

Note: Yarn is used double strand throughout.

Hat

Pattern
Row 1: Knit 15 with Color A, knit 15 with Color
B. Knit across row, being sure to twist yarn
when changing from Color A to Color B to avoid
making a hole in work.
Row 2: With Color A, purl 7, knit 1, purl 7, twist
yarn, with Color B purl 7, knit 1, purl 7.

Hat
Using #17 needles and Color A, cast on 15
stitches, then cast on 15 stitches with Color B.
Repeat Rows 1 and 2 for 16 rows. On next row,
purl 2 together across row, still following color
pattern, break yarn, leaving a long end. Draw
this yarn through remaining stitches.

Finishing
With contrasting colors, work 1 row single crochet over the garter-stitch ribs. Work 1 row
single crochet around bottom of hat. Do not
break yarn. Chain 1, work 1 row single crochet
backwards over stitches just worked, end off.

Scarf

Pattern
Row 1: Knit across row.
Row 2: Purl 7, knit 1, purl 7.

Scarf
Using #17 needles and Color A, cast on 15
stitches. Repeat Rows 1 and 2 for 16 rows. Continue to alternate Colors A and B, for 16 rows,
until you have 7 color squares worked, ending
with Color A. Bind off.

Finishing
Fringe each end, using both colors.

Two-Toned Hat and Scarf Set
Three skeins of yarn in each of two colors are all you
need to make this set.

Woman's Nubby, Long Vest

Women's Sizes
Directions are for small size. Changes for medium and large sizes are in parentheses.

Materials
2 (2, 2) skeins (8 oz or 224 g each) Sheep's Coat Yarn by Lily Mills or any bulky yarn to give gauge

Needles
#15
#10½ or #K crochet hook

Gauge
2½ stitches = 1 inch (2.5 cm)

Back
With #15 needles, cast on 42 (44, 47) stitches. Work garter stitch (knit every row) for 2 inches (5 cm), then work in stockinette stitch (knit 1 row, purl 1 row) till 18 (19, 20) inches (45, 47.5, 50 cm) or desired length to armhole. At the beginning of the next 2 rows, bind off 4 stitches, then decrease 1 stitch each side, every other row 3 (4, 4) times. Work even till armhole measures 8 (8½, 9) inches (20, 21.3, 22.5 cm). At the beginning of the next 2 rows, bind off 8 (8, 9) stitches, bind off remaining stitches.

Left Front
Cast on 26 (27, 28) stitches. Work garter stitch for 2 inches (5 cm), then work in stockinette stitch, keeping the 5 stitches at front edge in garter stitch. Work to armhole. Shape arm side same as for Back, and at the same time, decrease 1 stitch at front, making decreases inside border, every 4th row. Work till 13 (13, 14) stitches remain. Work even to shoulder, bind off 8 (8, 9) stitches from arm side, continue on 5 border stitches for 2½ inches more (6.3 cm), bind off.

Right Front
Work same as Left Front, reversing shaping.

Finishing
Sew shoulder seams. Sew tab of border to back of neck. Sew underarm seams. Work 1 row of single crochet around armhole. Do not block.

Woman's Nubby, Long Vest
The outstanding feature of this vest is its yarn. Yet, for an altogether different look, substitute the nubby yarn for a bulky yarn.

Boy's Shoulder-Buttoned Pullover
The stitching pattern of this sweater becomes rhythmic in no time at all. The sheen of the yarn and the button chosen for the shoulder give a more formal look to the sweater. For a more casual look use a different yarn and perhaps wooden buttons.

Boy's Shoulder-Buttoned Pullover

See photograph on facing page.

Boys' Sizes
Directions are for size 6. Changes for sizes 8 and 10 are in parentheses.

Materials
3 (4, 4) skeins (4 oz or 112 g each) Apollo by Plymouth or any bulky yarn to give gauge
2 ¾-inch buttons

Needles
#13
#15
#10½ crochet hook

Gauge
5 stitches = 2 inches (5 cm)

Note: Yarn is used double strand throughout.

Pattern
Row 1: *Knit 3, purl 1, knit 1, purl 1, repeat from * across Row 1. (For size 8 only end with knit 3.)
Row 2: (For size 8 only begin with purl 1, knit 1, purl 1.) *Knit 3, purl 1, knit 1, purl 1, repeat from * across row. (See close-up photograph.)

Back
With #13 needles cast on 24 (27, 30) stitches. Knit 1, purl 1 in ribbing for 2 inches (5 cm). Change to #15 needles and work pattern till 12 (13, 14) inches (30, 32.5, 35 cm) from beginning. Mark for armholes. Continue in pattern for 6 (6½, 7) inches (15, 16.3, 17.5 cm) more. At the beginning of the next 2 rows, bind off 8 (9, 10) stitches. Bind off remaining stitches.

Front
Work same as Back. Sew shoulder ½ inch (1.25 cm) from each side.

Sleeves
Using #15 needles, pick up 21 (24, 27) stitches along armhole. Work pattern till 12 (13, 14) inches (30, 32.5, 35 cm). Change to #13 needles, knit 1, purl 1 in ribbing for 2 inches (5 cm). Bind off in ribbing.

Finishing
Work 1 row single crochet around neck and shoulder, making 2 buttonloops on each shoulder. Sew 2 buttons each side.

Close-up view of stitching pattern of Boy's Shoulder-Buttoned Pullover.

Woman's Poncho Jacket

See photograph on facing page.

Women's Sizes
Directions are for small size. Changes for medium and large sizes are in parentheses.

Materials
8 skeins (3½ oz or 100 g each) Vail Homespun by Brunswick or any bulky yarn to give gauge
2 large buttons

Needles
#17
#10½ crochet hook

Gauge
2 stitches = 1 inch (2.5 cm)

Note: Yarn is used double strand throughout.

Back
With #17 needles, cast on 32 (36, 40) stitches.
Row 1: Purl 1, increase 1 stitch in next stitch, purl to last 2 stitches, increase 1 stitch in next stitch, purl 1.
Row 2: Knit 1, increase 1 stitch in next stitch, knit all across row to last 2 stitches, increase 1 stitch in next stitch, knit 1. Repeat Rows 1 and 2, 3 times more. There are now 48 (52, 56) stitches on needle. Work even in stockinette stitch (knit 1 row, purl 1 row) till 12 inches (30 cm) from the beginning, ending with a purl row. Next row, knit 1, increase 1 stitch in the next stitch, knit all across row till last 2 stitches, increase 1 stitch in the next stitch, knit 1. Next row, purl 1 stitch, increase 1 stitch in next stitch, purl across to last 2 stitches, increase 1 stitch in next stitch, purl 1. Repeat the last 2 rows once more.

There are now 56 (60, 64) stitches on needle. At the beginning of the next 2 rows, cast on 12 (14, 16) stitches. Continue in pattern as established on all 80 (88, 96) stitches till 9 inches (22.5 cm) from the cast-on stitches. At the beginning of the next 6 rows, bind off 10 (11, 12) stitches. Bind off remaining stitches.

Right Front
Cast on 16 (18, 20) stitches.
Row 1: Purl to last 2 stitches, increase 1 stitch in next stitch, purl last stitch.
Row 2: Knit 1, increase 1 stitch in next stitch, knit to end of row. Repeat Rows 1 and 2 3 times more. There are now 24 (26, 28) stitches on needle. Work even in stockinette stitch till 12 inches (30 cm) from beginning, ending with a purl row. Next row, increase 1 stitch in next stitch, knit across row. Next row, purl to last 2 stitches, increase 1 stitch in next stitch, purl 1. Repeat last 2 rows once more. There are now 28 (30, 32) stitches on needle. At the beginning of the next row, cast on 12 (14, 16) stitches. Knit these cast-on stitches, then finish row. Continue pattern as established till 9 inches (22.5 cm) from cast-on stitches, ending with a knit row. Shape neck and shoulders as follows:
Row 1: At neck edge and working in purl, bind off 7 stitches, finish row.
Row 2: Working in knit, bind off 10 (11, 12) stitches (arm side), work to last 2 stitches, knit last 2 stitches together (decrease).
Continuing in this manner, bind off 10 (11, 12) stitches from arm side 2 times more, and, at the same time, decrease 1 stitch at neck edge, every row, 2 (3, 4) times more.

Woman's Poncho Jacket
T-shaped garments like this one are quite simple and fun to do. You simply add on stitches at the armhole and continue across. Then the front piece and back piece are sewn together.

Left Front
Work same as Right Front, reversing all shaping.

Finishing
Sew shoulder seams from right side, letting the last stitch form a decorative ridge. Sew underarm seams from wrong side, to beginning of shaping. Starting at right underarm seam and with right side facing you, using a #10½ crochet hook, work 1 row single crochet around entire outside edge of poncho. Work 1 row single crochet around sleeves. Sew 2 large buttons in place, using space between the single crochet row and the knitted edge for buttonholes.

Woman's Curly, Cap-Sleeved Vest

Women's Sizes
Directions are for small size. Changes for medium and large sizes are in parentheses.

Materials
8 (8, 8) skeins (2 oz or 56 g each) Curlama by Stanley Berocco or any curly yarn to give gauge

Needles
#10½
#10½ crochet hook

Gauge
5 stitches = 2 inches (5 cm)

Back
With #10½ needles, cast on 42 (44, 46) stitches. Work in stockinette stitch (knit 1 row, purl 1 row), till 14 (14½, 15) inches (35, 36.3, 37.5 cm) or desired length to armhole. At the beginning of the next 2 rows, cast on 4 stitches. Work even on 50 (52, 54) stitches till 7 (7½, 8) inches (17.5, 18.8, 20 cm) from cast-on stitches. At the beginning of the next 4 rows, bind off 9 stitches. Bind off remaining 14 (16, 18) stitches.

Left Front
Cast on 22 stitches. Work in stockinette stitch till same length as back to armhole. At arm side, cast on 4 stitches. Continuing in stockinette stitch and keeping arm side even, decrease 1 stitch at neck edge. Repeat this neck decrease every 4th row till 18 stitches remain. Work even till shoulder, bind off 9 stitches twice from arm side.

Right Front
Work same as Left Front, reversing arm and neck shaping.

Finishing
Using purl side as right side, sew shoulder seams. Sew side seams. Work 1 row single crochet around all edges. Do not block.

Woman's Curly Cap-Sleeved Vest
Here a curly yarn added textural interest to a basic stockinette stitch. The cap sleeves are made by casting on stitches at the armhole. For a tunic version of this vest see page 65.

Woman's Curly, Cap-Sleeved Tunic

Finishing

Using purl side as right side of work, sew shoulder seams. Sew side seams. Work 1 row single crochet around neck, armhole, and bottom. Do not block.

Women's Sizes

Directions are for small size. Changes for medium and large sizes are in parentheses.

Materials

8 (8, 8) skeins (2 oz or 56 g each) Curlama by Stanley Berocco or any curly yarn to give gauge

Needles

#10½
#10½ crochet hook

Gauge

5 stitches = 2 inches (5 cm)

Back

With #10½ needles cast on 42 (44, 46) stitches. Work in stockinette stitch (knit 1 row, purl 1 row) till 14 (14½, 15) inches (35, 36.3, 37.8 cm) or desired length to armhole. At the beginning of the next 2 rows, cast on 4 stitches. Work even on 50 (52, 54) stitches till 7 (7½, 8) inches (17.5, 18.8, 20 cm) from the cast-on stitches. At the beginning of the next 4 rows, bind off 9 stitches. Bind off remaining stitches.

Front

Work same as Back till armhole measures 5 (5½, 6) inches (12.5, 13.8, 15 cm) from the cast-on stitches. Work neck shaping as follows: Work across 22 stitches, join new yarn, and bind off center 6 (8, 10) stitches very loosely. Continue to work remaining 22 stitches. Working both sides of front, each with separate yarn, decrease 1 stitch each neck edge, every row, 4 times. Work even if necessary till 7 (7½, 8) inches (17.5, 18.8, 20 cm) from the cast-on stitches. Bind off 9 stitches twice from each arm side.

Finishing

Using purl side as right side of work, sew shoulder seams. Sew side seams. Work 1 row single crochet around neck, armhole, and bottom. Do not block.

Woman's Curly Cap-Sleeved Tunic
This basic pullover, which can be made very quickly, is a perfect addition to any woman's wardrobe. It can dress up a basic outfit as shown here. Directions for the vest version of this tunic are on page 64.

Woman's Puff-Trimmed Vest
Vests make perfect gifts because of their versatility, and "weekend" vests are the best kind. This pattern is simply two repeated rows. The puff trim is done by basically pulling yarn through loops on the needles.

Woman's Puff-Trimmed Vest

Women's Sizes
Directions are for small size. Changes for medium and large sizes are in parentheses.

Materials
4 (4, 5) skeins (1½ oz or 40 g each) Majestic Mohair by Galler or any mohair yarn to give gauge

Needles
#15
#8 or #H crochet hook

Gauge
2½ stitches = 1 inch (2.5 cm)

Back
With #15 needles, cast on 31 stitches. Work pattern as follows:
Row 1: Knit 1 *purl 5, knit 1, repeat from * across.
Row 2: Purl 1, * knit 5, purl 1, repeat from * across row.
Repeat the 2 pattern rows for 16 (17, 17) inches (40, 42.5, 42.5 cm) or desired length from waist to shoulder. At the beginning of the next 2 rows, bind off 8 stitches. Bind off remaining stitches.

Left Front
Cast on 16 stitches. Work pattern as follows:
Row 1: Knit 1, *purl 5, knit 1, repeat from * ending row with purl 3.
Row 2: Knit 3, *purl 1, knit 5, repeat from * ending row with purl 1.
Repeat these 2 rows till 12 (13, 13) inches (30, 32.5, 32.5 cm) or 4 inches (10 cm) less than Back to shoulder, ending at front edge. Bind off 4 stitches at neck edge, then decrease 1 stitch same edge every other row, 4 times. Work even to shoulder, bind off remaining stitches.

Right Front
Work same as Left Front, reversing pattern and shaping.

Side Pieces *(make 2)*
Cast on 23 stitches. Work pattern as follows:
Row 1: Knit 5 *purl 1, knit 5, repeat from * across row.
Row 2: Purl 5, *knit 1, purl 5, repeat from * across row.
Repeat these 2 pattern rows for 4 (5, 6) inches (10, 12.5, 15 cm), bind off.

Finishing
Sew shoulder seams. Sew side pieces in place, starting at bottom up to armhole to form body of vest. Starting at right underarm seam, right side facing you, work 1 row of single crochet around entire outside edge of vest. Join with a slip stitch to start. Chain 3, skip 1 stitch, make 1 half double crochet in next stitch, chain 3, work 1 puff stitch over the bar of the half double crochet (see directions below), *skip 2 stitches, make 1 half double crochet in next stitch, chain 3, make 1 puff stitch over the bar of the half double crochet, repeat from * all around, join with a slip stitch to starting chain 3, end off. Work same pattern around both armholes. Block gently, by steaming wrong side out with a pressing cloth.

Make puff stitch as follows: (yarn over hook, pickup a loop) 3 times, yarn over, pull through all but last loop on hook, yarn over, pull through last loop.

Woman's Tie-Front Vest
A beautiful soft vest can be made in a jiffy. Once you know
how to add on the ties, you might want to add them to other
"weekend" vests.

Woman's Tie-Front Vest

See photograph on facing page.

Women's Sizes
One size fits all.

Materials
5 skeins (1½ oz or 40 g each) Majestic Mohair by Galler or any mohair yarn to give gauge

Needles
#11
#15

Gauge
1½ stitches = 1 inch (2.5 cm)

Note: Yarn is used double strand throughout.

Back
With #11 needles, cast on 24 stitches. Work in knit 1, purl 1 ribbing for 2 inches (5 cm). Change to #15 needles and work in stockinette stitch (knit 1 row, purl 1 row), increasing 1 stitch each side, every 2 inches (5 cm) 2 times. Work till 8 inches (20 cm) from the beginning or desired length to underarm. At the beginning of the next 2 rows, bind off 2 stitches. Work even until armhole measures 8 inches (20 cm). At the beginning of the next 4 rows, bind off 4 stitches. Bind off remaining stitches.

Right Front
With #11 needles, cast on 30 stitches.
Row 1: Knit 18 stitches, knit 1, purl 1 in ribbing to end of row.
Row 2: Purl 1, knit 1 in ribbing for 12 stitches, purl to end of row.
Repeat Rows 1 and 2 for 2 inches (5 cm), ending with Row 2. Bind off 18 stitches of stockinette stitch. Change to #15 needles and work in stockinette stitch, increasing 1 stitch at arm side every 2 inches (5 cm) 2 times. Work until piece measures 8 inches (20 cm) or desired length to underarm. At beginning of the next row, bind off 2 stitches at arm side. At the same time, decrease 1 stitch at neck edge, every 2 inches (5 cm), 4 times. Work till armhole measures 8 inches (20 cm). Bind off 4 stitches from arm side, 2 times.

Left Front
Work same as Right Front, reversing all shaping.

Finishing
Sew up side seams. Starting at upper right corner of tie, single crochet along top edge of tie, around the front edges, finishing at top of left tie. Single crochet around armhole.

Woman's Short, Curly Vest
Here's a vest you can sit down and finish in a few hours.
It's a simple stockinette stitch done with curly yarn.

70

Woman's Short, Curly Vest

See photograph on facing page.

Women's Sizes
Directions are for small size. Changes for medium and large sizes are in parentheses.

Materials
4 (4, 4) skeins (2 oz or 56 g each) Curlama by Stanley Berocco or any curly yarn to give gauge

Needles
#10½
#10½ crochet hook

Gauge
5 stitches = 2 inches (5 cm)

Back
With #10½ needles, cast on 35 (37, 39) stitches. Work in stockinette stitch (knit 1 row, purl 1 row) till 3 inches (7.5 cm) from beginning. Increase 1 stitch each side, and repeat this increase every 2 inches (5 cm), 2 times. There are now 41 (43, 45) stitches on needle. Work even till 8 (9, 9½) inches (20, 22.5, 23.8 cm) or desired length to underarm. At the beginning of the next 2 rows, bind off 4 stitches. Decrease 1 stitch each side every other row, 2 times. There are now 29 (31, 33) stitches on needle. Work even till armhole is 7½ (8, 8½) inches (18.8, 20, 21.3 cm). Work across 10 (11, 12) stitches, join new ball of yarn, bind off center 9 stitches, work remaining 10 (11, 12) stitches. Continue in stockinette stitch, decreasing 1 stitch each neck edge, every row, 3 times. Bind off remaining 14 (16, 18) stitches.

Left Front
Cast on 10 (11, 12) stitches. Work in stockinette stitch, increasing 1 stitch front edge every row, 10 times. Work even on the 20 (21, 22) stitches till 3 inches (7.5 cm) from beginning. Increase 1 stitch at arm side and repeat the increase every 2 inches (5 cm) 2 times. Work even till 8 (9, 9½) inches (20, 22.5, 23.8 cm) or desired length to underarm. At arm side, bind off 4 stitches. Decrease 1 stitch arm side, every other row twice. Work till armhole measures 7½ (8, 8½) inches (18.8, 20, 21.3 cm), decreasing every 4th row till 7 (8, 9) stitches remain. Bind off.

Right Front
Work same as Left Front, reversing all shaping.

Finishing
Using purl side as right side, sew shoulder seams. Sew side seams. With #10½ crochet hook and starting at right underarm seam, work 1 row single crochet all around outside edges of garment. Starting at underarm seam, work 1 row single crochet around each armhole. To block curly or heavy-textured yarn, wet thoroughly in cool water, remove excess water by rolling in towels, and lay flat to dry, "pressing" into shape with fingers.

Boy's Striped, Shawl-Collared Cardigan
The front bands and collar of this cardigan are knitted
separately and then sewn on.

Boy's Striped, Shawl-Collared Cardigan

See photograph on facing page.

Boys' Sizes
Directions are for size 4. Changes for sizes 6 and 8 are in parentheses.

Materials
3 (4, 4) skeins (3½ oz or 100 g each) Nova by Plymouth in Color A or any bulky yarn to give gauge
2 (3, 3) skeins in Color B
4 buttons

Needles
#10½
#15

Gauge
2 stitches = 1 inch (2.5 cm)

Note: Yarn is used double strand throughout. Purl side is right side.

Striping Pattern
4 rows Color A.
6 rows Color B.
2 rows Color A.
2 rows Color B.
2 rows Color A.
6 rows Color B.

Back
With #10½ needles, cast on 32 (34, 36) stitches with Color A. Knit 1, purl 1 in ribbing for 1 inch (2.5 cm). Change to #15 needles and work stockinette stitch in striping pattern until 14 (15, 16) inches (35, 37.5, 40 cm) or desired length to underarm. At the beginning of the next 2 rows, bind off 2 stitches. Continue working in striping pattern, decreasing 1 stitch each side, every other row, till 12 stitches remain. Work 2 rows even, bind off.

Front
Cast on 16 (17, 18) stitches and work same as Back till armhole. Shape arm sides same as for Back. Continue as for Back and, at the same time, decrease 1 stitch each neck edge, every 6th row. Continue in this manner till 2 stitches remain, bind off.

Sleeves
Cast on 18 (19, 20) stitches and work same as Back, increasing 1 stitch each side every 3 inches (7.5 cm), 1 (2, 3) time. Work even till 14 (15, 16) inches (35, 37.5, 40 cm) or desired length to underarm. At the beginning of the next 2 rows, bind off 2 stitches, then decrease 1 stitch each side every 4th row, 3 times, then every other row till same length as Back. Bind off.

Front Bands and Collar
For the right front band: cast on 5 stitches with Color A. Work in garter stitch (knit each row) for same length as Front to start of neck shaping. Then increase 1 stitch on inside edge of collar and repeat this increase every row till collar is 18 (20, 22) stitches wide. Work even for 8 (9, 9) inches (20, 22.5, 22.5 cm) more, bind off. For the left front band: Work same as for right front, reversing shaping and evenly spacing 5 buttonholes between bottom and start of collar shaping. To make button holes: Knit 2, bind off 1 stitch, knit next 2 stitches. On next row, cast 1 stitch over bound-off stitch, and continue garter stitch as established.

Girl's Tyrolean-Yoked Cardigan
Another way to add interest to a basic sweater is to change the textures. The body of this sweater is done in stockinette stitch, while the yoke and sleeves are done in reverse stockinette stitch. The yoke is further set off by an embroidered flower. Choose any shape and any other color yarn you like for the embroidery. For the pullover version of this sweater see page 76.

Girl's Tyrolean-Yoked Cardigan

See photograph on facing page.

Girls' Sizes
Directions are for size 4. Changes for sizes 6 and 8 are in parentheses.

Materials
7 (8, 9) skeins (4 oz or 112 g each) Big Berella Bulky by Bernat or any bulky yarn to give gauge
small amount in Color B
separating zipper

Needles
#15
#10½ crochet hook

Gauge
2½ stitches = 1 inch (2.5 cm)

Back
With #15 needles, cast on 30 (32, 34) stitches. Work in stockinette stitch (knit 1 row, purl 1 row) till 8 (9, 10) inches (20, 22.5, 25 cm) from beginning or desired length to armhole. Work in reverse stockinette stitch (purl side is right side) and, at the beginning of the next 2 rows, bind off 2 (3, 3) stitches. Work even till armhole is 5½ (6, 6½) inches (13.8, 15, 16.3 cm). At the beginning of the next 2 rows, bind off 8 stitches, place remaining stitches on holder.

Left Front
Cast on 15 (16, 17) stitches. Work same as Back till 8 (9, 10) inches (20, 22.5, 25 cm) or desired length to armhole. Bind off 2 stitches arm side of next row and work in reverse stockinette stitch till armhole measures 3½ (4, 4½) inches, (8.8, 10, 11.3 cm) ending at front edge. Bind off

3 stitches, then decrease 1 stitch front edge every row, 2 (3, 4) times. Work even to shoulder, bind off remaining stitches.

Sleeves
Cast on 16 (18, 20) stitches. Work in reverse stockinette stitch, increasing 1 stitch each side every 3 inches (7.5 cm), 3 times. Work even till 9 (10, 11) inches (22.5, 25, 27.5 cm) or desired length. At the beginning of the next 2 rows, bind off 2 (3, 3) stitches. Then decrease 1 stitch each side every other row, till 10 stitches remain, bind off.

Neckband
Starting at right front, pick up 30 (32, 34) stitches around neck. Work in reverse stockinette stitch for 4 rows, bind off.

Finishing
Sew seams. Using Color B, work 1 row single crochet along each front edge and around sleeve edge. Embroider flower on right front, as shown in photograph. Sew in zipper. Do not block. The sweater in the photograph is decorated with small ladybug buttons. These can be easily obtained in variety stores.

Girl's Tyrolean-Yoked Pullover

Girls' Sizes

Directions are for size 4. Changes for sizes 6 and 8 are in parentheses.

Materials

7 (8, 9) skeins (4 oz or 112 g each) Big Berella Bulky by Bernat in Color A or any bulky yarn to give gauge
small amount in Color B

Needles

#15

Gauge

2½ stitches = 1 inch (2.5 cm)

Back

With #15 needles, cast on 30 (32, 34) stitches. Work in stockinette stitch (knit 1 row, purl 1 row) till 8 (9, 10) inches (20, 22.5, 25 cm) from beginning or desired length to armhole. Work in reverse stockinette stitch (purl side is right side) and, at the beginning of the next 2 rows, bind off 2 (3, 3) stitches. Work even till armhole is 5½ (6, 6½) inches (13.8, 15, 16.3 cm). At the beginning of the next 2 rows, bind off 8 stitches, place remaining stitches on a holder.

Front

Work same as Back till armhole is 3½ (4, 5) inches (8.8, 10, 12.5 cm). Work across 9 (9, 10) stitches, place center 8 stitches on a holder, join new yarn, work remaining 9 (9, 10) stitches. Now, working both sides at once, each with separate yarn, decrease 1 stitch each neck edge, every row, 1 (1, 2) time. Work even to shoulder, bind off remaining 8 stitches.

Girl's Tyrolean-Yoked Pullover
The pullover version of the sweater shown on page 74.

Sleeves

Cast on 16 (18, 20) stitches. Work in reverse stockinette stitch, increasing 1 stitch each side every 3 inches (7.5 cm), 3 times. Work even till 9 (10, 11) inches (22.5, 25, 27.5 cm) or desired length. At the beginning of the next 2 rows, bind off 2 (3, 3) stitches. Decrease 1 stitch each side every other row, till 10 stitches remain, bind off.

Finishing

Sew one shoulder seam, with right side facing you. Pick up 30 (32, 34) stitches around neck. Work reverse stockinette stitch for 4 rows, bind off. Sew seams, do not block. Embroider flower on yoke, following photograph.

Girl's Multicolored Tunic

Girls' Sizes

Directions are for small size. Changes for medium and large sizes are in parentheses.

Materials

3 (4, 4) skeins (4 oz or 112 g each) Variegated Apollo by Plymouth or any textured yarn to give gauge

Needles

#17
#10½ crochet hook

Gauge

2 stitches = 1 inch (2.5 cm)

Note: Yarn is used double strand throughout.

Back

With #17 needles, cast on 23 (25, 27) stitches. Work in seed stitch (knit 1, purl 1 each row--not ribbing) for 6 rows. Continue in stockinette stitch (knit 1 row, purl 1 row) till 10 (12, 14) inches (25, 30, 35 cm) from beginning. At the beginning of the next 2 rows, cast on 9 (11, 13) stitches. There are now 41 (47, 53) stitches on the needle. Work even till 4 (4½, 5) inches (10, 11.3, 12.5 cm) from cast-on stitches. Work across 14 (16, 18) stitches, join new ball of yarn, bind off next 13 (15, 17) stitches. Work remaining 14 (16, 18) stitches. Working each side with separate yarn, continue in stockinette stitch till 6 (6½, 7) inches (15, 16.3, 17.5 cm) from cast-on stitches. Bind off all remaining stitches.

Girl's Multicolored Tunic
Variegated yarns are a great way to add interest to a basic pattern or stitch. The tunic is a simple T shape. The front and back pieces are identical.

Front

Work same as Back.

Finishing

Sew shoulder seams, catching underside of stitch and allowing bind-off to show, forming the saddle shoulder. Sew underarm seams. With the #10½ crochet hook, work 1 row single crochet around neck edge, join with a slip stitch to beginning, do not turn. Chain 1, work 1 row of single crochet backwards over the stitches just worked. Work 1 row single crochet around armholes. Block by steaming gently, wrong side out.

Child's Hooded Sweatshirt

See photograph on facing page.

Children's Sizes
Directions are for size 4. Changes for sizes 6 and 8 are in parentheses.

Materials
5 (6, 7) skeins (3½ oz or 110 g each) Vail Homespun by Brunswick or any bulky yarn to give gauge
zipper

Needles
#15
#17
#10½ or K crochet hook

Gauge
2 stitches = 1 inch (2.5 cm)

Note: Yarn is used double strand throughout.
This garment is worked in one piece from the hood down to the bottom.

Hood and Yoke
Starting at hood, cast on 31 (33, 35) stitches.
Row 1: Knit across row.
Row 2: Knit 2, purl to last 2 stitches, knit 2.
Repeat Rows 1 and 2 for 9½ (10, 11) inches (23.8, 25, 27.5 cm), ending on a knit row. Change to #15 needles and work ribbing pattern as follows: Next row, knit 2, *purl 1, knit 1, repeat from * across row, ending with knit 2. Next row, knit 2, *knit 1, purl 1, repeat from * across row, ending knit 2. Repeat last 2 rows once more. Change back to #17 needles and work as follows:
Row 1 (wrong side): Knit 2, purl 5 (5, 6), place marker on needle, purl 3 (4, 4), place marker on needle, purl 11, place marker on needle, purl 3 (4, 4), place marker on needle, purl 5 (5, 6), knit last 2 stitches.

Row 2: Knit all across row, increasing 1 stitch before and after each marker (8 increases made).
Row 3: Knit 2, purl across row, slipping markers as you work, to last 2 stitches, knit last 2 stitches.
Repeat Rows 2 and 3 till there are 22 (24, 26) stitches on center back section of work. End with a knit row. Next row, work to 1st marker, slip these stitches to a holder, remove marker, work to 3rd marker, slip the stitches between the 2nd and 3rd marker to a holder, work to 4th marker, slip remaining stitches not worked onto a holder, leave a marker on this holder. You now have 2 sleeve sections on the needle.

Sleeves
Both sleeves will be worked at the same time, each with separate strands of yarn. Decrease 1 stitch each side of each sleeve every 3 inches (7.5 cm) 2 (3, 3) times. Work even till sleeve is 7 (8, 9) inches (17.5, 18.8, 22.5 cm) from underarm. Change to #15 needles. Knit 1, purl 1 in ribbing for 3 inches, bind off in ribbing.

Body
Join yarn at underarm by holder with marker, purl across this section, keeping the 2 stitches at end in garter stitch as established. Knit across this same section, knit across back section, knit other front section. You now have 3 body sections on needle to be worked as 1 piece. Continue pattern as established till 7 (8, 9) inches (17.5, 20, 22.5 cm) or desired length. Change to #15 needles. Work knit 1, purl 1 ribbing for 3 inches (7.5 cm). Bind off in ribbing.

Child's Hooded Sweatshirt
What child could not use a basic sweater such as this one in his or her wardrobe; and it can be made in just a few hours.

Pocket

Cast on 10 stitches. Work stockinette stitch for 6 rows. Bind off 2 stitches on 1 side only, decrease same side every other row, till 2 stitches remain, bind off. Work other pocket in the same way, reversing shaping. Sew underarm seams. Work 1 row single crochet around pockets. Sew in place. Work 1 row single crochet along each front edge. Sew in zipper. Do not block.

Girl's Car Coat

See photograph on facing page.

Girls' Sizes
Directions are for size 4. Changes for sizes 6 and 8 are in parentheses.

Materials
7 (8, 9) skeins (4 oz or 112 g each) Big Berella Bulky by Bernat or any bulky yarn to give gauge
6 toggle buttons
snap

Needles
#15
#10½ crochet hook

Gauge
2½ stitches = 1 inch (2.5 cm)

Pattern (triple seed stitch)
Row 1: *Knit 1, purl 1, repeat from * across row.
Row 2: Work same as Row 1.
Row 3: Work same as Row 1.
Row 4: *Purl 1, knit 1, repeat from * across row.
Row 5: Work same as Row 4.
Row 6: Work same as Row 4.
Repeat these 6 rows for pattern.

Back
Cast on 30 (32, 34) stitches. Work triple seed stitch pattern till 10 (11, 12) inches (25, 27.5, 30 cm) or desired length to underarm. At the beginning of the next 2 rows, bind off 2 (3, 3) stitches. Work even till armhole is 5½ (6, 6½) inches (13.8, 15, 16.3 cm). At the beginning of the next 2 rows, bind off 8 stitches. Place remaining stitches on holder.

Left Front
Cast on 20 (22, 24) stitches. Work pattern same as Back to armhole, ending at arm side. Bind off 2 (3, 3) stitches at armhole. Work even till 4 (4½, 5) inches (10, 11.3, 12.5 cm) from armhole, ending at front edge. Bind off 7 (8, 9) stitches at front edge. Decrease same edge every row, 3 (3, 4) times. Work even to shoulder and bind off remaining stitches.

Right Front
Work same as Left Front, reversing all shaping.

Sleeves
Cast on 20 (22, 24) stitches. Work in pattern as established, increasing 1 stitch each side every 3 inches (7.5 cm), 3 times. Work even till 12 (13, 14) inches (30, 32.5, 35 cm) from beginning (this allows for 3-inch turn-back cuff.) At the beginning of the next 2 rows, bind off 2 (3, 3) stitches. Then decrease 1 stitch each side every other row, till 8 stitches remain, bind off.

Collar
With #15 needles, right side facing you, and starting 4 (5, 5) stitches in from front edge, pick up 30 (32, 34) stitches around neck. Work in pattern for 3 (7.5 cm) inches, bind off loosely.

Finishing
Sew seams. Starting at right front, right side facing you, work 1 row single crochet around collar. Starting at same point, work 1 row single crochet down front, around bottom, and up other front. Work 1 row single crochet around cuff. Do not block. Sew a snap to upper end of front and under collar.

Girl's Car Coat
The stitching pattern and frogs make this coat just fancy enough to wear for a visit. The stitching pattern consists of six repeated rows.

Frogs

With 1 strand of yarn, cast on 4 stitches. * Slip the stitches to other end of needle, carry yarn tightly across at back of work, and knit 1 row. Repeat from * until 9 inches (22.5 cm) from the beginning when stretched, forming a tube of stockinette stitches. Slip stitches to other end of needle and bind off. Weave ends together.

Fold and form 1-inch (2.5-cm) button loop by sewing seam to other side of frog. Wind yarn around over seam and fasten. Finish other side to correspond. Sew onto coat as pictured. Make 3 frogs altogether.

Woman's Chanel-Type Tweed Jacket, Hat, and Scarf Set

See photograph on facing page.

Women's Sizes
Directions are for small size. Changes for medium and large sizes are in parentheses.

Materials
9 skeins (3½ oz or 110 g each) Vail Homespun by Brunswick in Color A or any bulky yarn to give gauge
9 skeins in Color B
large hook and eye (optional)

Needles
#17
#10½ crochet hook

Gauge
2 stitches = 1 inch (2.5 cm)

Note: Yarn is used one strand of each color held together throughout.

Back
With #17 needles, cast on 34 (36, 38) stitches. Work in stockinette stitch (knit 1 row, purl 1 row) till 11 (12, 13) inches (27.5, 30, 32.5 cm) or desired length from beginning. End on a purl row. At the beginning of the next 2 rows, bind off 2 stitches. Work even till armhole is 8 (8½, 9) inches (18.8, 21.3, 22.5 cm). At the beginning of the next 2 rows, bind off 10 stitches. Bind off remaining stitches.

Left Front
Cast on 18 (19, 20) stitches. Work in stockinette stitch till armhole. At arm side, bind off 2 stitches. Work even till 6 (6½, 7) inches (15, 16.3, 17.5 cm), ending at front edge. At front edge, bind off 4 (5, 6) stitches. Decrease 1 stitch front edge every row, 2 times. Work even to shoulder, bind off remaining stitches.

Right Front
Work same as Left Front, reversing all shaping.

Sleeves
Sew shoulder seams. With right side facing you, pick up 26 (28, 30) stitches along armhole edge. Work in stockinette stitch, decreasing 1 stitch each side every 4 inches (10 cm), 4 times. Work even till 18 (19, 20) inches (45, 47.5, 50 cm), bind off.

Finishing
Sew underarm seams. With #10½ crochet hook, starting at bottom right underarm seam, work 1 row single crochet around entire outside edge of garment, making 3 single crochets in each corner to turn. Work around to where you started, do not break yarn. Do not turn. Working backwards, fairly loosely, work 1 row single crochet over stitches just worked. Work same edging around sleeves. Use large hook and eyes for closing if desired. Do not block ·

Hat

With 1 strand of each yarn held together and #17 needles, cast on 44 stitches. Knit 1, purl 1 in ribbing for 4 inches (10 cm). Work in stockinette stitch for 4 inches (10 cm) ending with a purl row. Next row, *knit 3, knit 2 together, repeat from * across row. Purl 1 row. Next row, *knit 2, knit 2 together, repeat from * across row. Purl 1 row. Next row, knit 2 together all across row. Break yarn, leaving a long end for sewing. Pull this end through remaining stitches and gather together. Sew back seam with same end, weaving ribbed border so that it may be turned up if desired. Do not block.

Woman's Chanel-Type Tweed Jacket, Hat, and Scarf Set
This tweed jacket is set off by its matching scarf and hat.

Scarf

With 1 strand of each yarn held together and #17 needles, cast on 18 stitches. Work in stockinette stitch for 60 inches (150 cm), bind off. Cut yarn into 10-inch (25-cm) lengths. Pull through each stitch at ends for fringe. Scarf will roll slightly to give tubular look. Do not block.

Woman's Sand-Stitch Pullover
We combined soft, fluffy yarn and big needles with the versatile sand stitch to give this V pullover its softly textured look.

84

Woman's Sand-Stitch Pullover

See photograph on facing page. This sweater can also be made for a man. See directions on page 87.

Women's Sizes
Directions are for small size. Changes for medium and large are in parentheses.

Materials
10 (12, 14) skeins (1½ oz or 40 g each) Frostlon Petite by Spinnerin or any mohair yarn to give gauge

Needles
#15
#17

Gauge
2 stitches = 1 inch (2.5 cm)

Note: Yarn is worked double strand throughout.

Pattern
Row 1: Knit all across row.
Row 2: Knit 1, *purl 1, knit 1, repeat from * across row.

Back
With #15 needles, cast on 32 (34, 36) stitches. Knit 1, purl 1 in ribbing for 10 rows. Change to #17 needles and work pattern till 12 (13, 14) inches (30, 32.5, 35 cm) or desired length to underarm. At the beginning of the next 2 rows, bind off 2 stitches. Continue in pattern till armhole is 7½ (8, 8½) inches (18.8, 20, 21.3 cm). At the beginning of the next 2 rows, bind off 10 stitches, place remaining stitches on a holder.

Front
Work same as Back till armhole bind-off is completed, then work across 14 (15, 16) stitches, place remaining 14 (15, 16) stitches on a holder. Continue in pattern, decreasing 1 stitch at front edge. Repeat the decrease every 4th row, 3 (4, 5) times more. Work even if necessary to shoulder, bind off. Joining yarn at center, work other side to correspond. Sew left shoulder seam, place stitches from back of neck on #15 needle. With right side facing you, pick up 20 stitches along left neck edge, place marker, pick up 1 stitch in center of V neck, place marker, pick up 20 stitches along other side. Work these stitches as follows: Knit 1, purl 1 in ribbing till 2 stitches before the center marker, slip 1 stitch, knit 1, pass the slipped stitch over the knit stitch, purl the center stitch, knit next 2 stitches together, purl 1, knit 1 in ribbing to end of row. Next row same, except knit the center stitch. Repeat the last 2 rows 1 more time, bind off in ribbing. Sew other shoulder seam.

Sleeves

With #17 needles, pick up 26 (28, 30) stitches along armhole and work sleeve in pattern for 5 inches (12.5 cm), decreasing 1 stitch each side. Work for 5 inches (12.5 cm) more, decrease again. Work even till 18 (19, 19½) inches (45, 47.5, 48.8 cm), decrease 4 stitches evenly spaced, across row. Change to #15 needles and knit 1, purl 1 in ribbing for 3 inches (7.5 cm), bind off in ribbing.

Finishing
Sew underarm seams. Do not block.

Man's Sand-Stitch Pullover
This sweater is perfect for men or women.

Man's Sand-Stitch Pullover

See photograph on facing page. This sweater can also be made for a woman. See directions on page 85.

Men's Sizes
Directions are for small size. Changes for medium and large are in parentheses.

Materials
14 (16, 18) skeins (1½ oz or 40 g each) Frostlon Petite by Spinnerin or any mohair yarn to give gauge

Needles
#15
#17

Gauge
2 stitches = 1 inch (2.5 cm)

Note: Yarn is worked double strand throughout.

Pattern
Row 1: Knit all across row.
Row 2: Knit 1, *purl 1, knit 1, repeat from * across row.

Back
With #15 needles, cast on 38 (40, 42) stitches. Knit 1, purl 1 in ribbing for 10 rows. Change to #17 needles and work pattern till 14½ (15, 15½) inches (36.3, 37.5, 38.8 cm) or desired length to underarm. At the beginning of the next 2 rows, bind off 3 stitches. Continue in pattern till armhole is 9 (9½, 10) inches (22.5, 23.8, 25 cm). At the beginning of the next 2 rows, bind off 12 stitches, place remaining stitches on a holder.

Front
Work same as Back till armhole bind-off is completed, then work across 17 (18, 19) stitches, place remaining 17 (18, 19) stitches on a holder. Continue in pattern, decreasing 1 stitch at front edge. Repeat the decrease every 4th row, 4 (5, 6) times more. Work even if necessary to shoulder, bind off. Joining yarn at center, work other side to correspond. Sew left shoulder seam, place stitches from back of neck on #15 needles. With right side facing you, pick up 22 stitches along left neck edge, place marker, pick up 1 stitch in center of V neck, place marker, pick up 22 stitches along other side. Work these stitches as follows: Knit 1, purl 1 in ribbing till 2 stitches before the center marker, slip 1 stitch, knit 1, pass the slipped stitch over the knit stitch, purl the center stitch, knit next 2 stitches together, purl 1, knit 1 in ribbing to end of row. Next row same, except knit the center stitch. Repeat the last 2 rows 1 more time, bind off in ribbing. Sew other shoulder seam.

Sleeves
With #17 needles, pick up 32 (34, 36) stitches along armhole and work sleeve in pattern for 5 inches (10 cm), decreasing 1 stitch each side. Work for 5 inches (10 cm) more, decrease again. Work even till 20 (20½, 21) inches (50, 51.3, 52.5 cm), decrease 4 stitches evenly spaced, across row. Change to #15 needles and knit 1, purl 1 in ribbing for 3 inches (7.5 cm), bind off in ribbing.

Finishing
Sew underarm seams. Do not block.

Woman's Spring Pullover
We combined three yarns to make this simply constructed
and perfect-for-spring sweater.

Woman's Spring Pullover

See photograph on facing page.

Women's Sizes
Directions are for small size. Changes for medium and large sizes are in parentheses.

Materials
5 (6, 6) skeins (3½ oz or 100 g each) Soho Bulky by Tahki or any bulky yarn to give gauge

6 (6, 7) skeins (2 oz or 56 g each) Nubs and Slubs by Stanley Berocco or any nubby yarn to give gauge

1 (2, 2) skeins (3½ oz or 100 g each) Combo Nevada by Plymouth or any bulky yarn to give gauge

Needles
#11 and #15

Gauge
2½ stitches = 1 inch (2.5 cm)

Note: Yarn is used single strand for borders (Combo Nevada), and double strand (1 strand Nubs and Slubs and 1 strand Soho Bulky) for body of garment.

Purl side is the right side.

Back
With #11 needles, cast on 46 (48, 50) stitches. Knit 1, purl 1 in ribbing for 2 inches (5 cm). Break border yarn, change to #15 needle, join 2 strands of body yarn. Knit the first 2 rows (this reverses the stockinette stitch), then continue in Purl 1 row, knit 1 row till 13 (14, 15) inches (32.5, 35, 37.5 cm) or desired length to underarm. At the beginning of the next 2 rows, bind off 2 stitches. Work even till armhole is 7 (7½, 8) inches (17.5, 18.8, 20 cm). At the beginning of the next 2 rows, bind off 6 stitches. Place remaining stitches on a holder.

Front
Work same as Back till armhole is 4 (4½, 5) inches (10, 11.3, 12.5 cm). Work across 9 stitches, place center 24 (26, 28) stitches on a holder, join new strands of same yarn, work remaining 9 stitches. Working on both sides at once, each with separate strands of yarn, decrease 1 stitch at each neck edge, every row, 3 times. Work even till armhole measures same as Back, bind off remaining stitches.

First Sleeves
Sew 1 shoulder, pick up 36 (38, 40) stitches along armhole edge, being sure to divide stitches equally on each side of shoulder seam. Continue in pattern as established for 16 (17, 18) inches (40, 42.5, 45 cm) or 3 inches (7.5 cm) less than desired length of sleeve (allow for some blousing). On next row, join border yarn and change to #11 needles. Knit, decreasing evenly across row to 22 (24, 26) stitches. Knit 1, purl 1 in ribbing for 3 inches (7.5 cm), bind off in ribbing.

Neckband
Starting at back by shoulder that is not sewn, with #11 needles and border yarn, pick up 66 (68, 70) stitches around neckline, including those on holders. Knit 1, purl 1 in ribbing for 1½ inches (3.8 cm), bind off in ribbing.

Second Sleeve
Sew other shoulder, work to correspond to first sleeve.

Finishing
Sew underarm seams. Do not block.

Man's Fisherman's Cable Pullover
Who says fisherman cables are complicated? This pullover
has a simple cable pattern that you'll enjoy working. For
the cardigan version of this sweater see page 92.

Man's Fisherman's Cable Pullover

See photograph on facing page.

Men's Sizes

Directions are for small size. Changes for medium and large sizes are in parentheses.

Materials

9 (9, 10) skeins (3½ oz or 100 g each) Vail Homespun by Brunswick or any bulky yarn to give gauge

Needles

#15
#17
1 bulky double-pointed cable needle
2 large stitch holders

Gauge

2 stitches = 1 inch (2.5 cm)

Note: Yarn is used double strand throughout.

Pattern

Row 1 (wrong side): *Knit 7 (9, 11), purl 1, knit 1, purl 6, knit 1, purl 1, repeat from * to last 7 (9, 11) stitches, knit to end of row.

Row 2 (right side): *Knit 1, purl 1 on first 7 (9, 11) stitches, knit 1, purl 1, knit 6, purl 1, knit 1, repeat from * to last 7 (9, 11) stitches, knit 1, purl 1 to end of row.

Row 3: Work same as Row 1.

Row 4 (cable row): *Knit 1, purl 1 on first 7 (9, 11) stitches, knit 1, purl 1, slip next 3 stitches onto cable needle and hold in back of work, knit next 3 stitches, then knit the 3 stitches from cable needle, purl 1, knit 1, repeat from * to last 7 (9, 11) stitches, knit 1, purl 1 to end of row.

Row 5: Work same as Row 1.

Row 6: Work same as Row 2.

Row 7: Work same as Row 1.

Row 8: Work same as Row 2.

Back

With #15 needles, cast on 41 (47, 53) stitches. Work in knit 1, purl 1 ribbing for 3 inches (7.5 cm). Change to #17 needles and work the 8 rows of pattern until piece measures 16 inches (40 cm) or desired length from start to underarm. At the beginning of the next 2 rows, bind off 2 stitches. Decrease 1 stitch each side, every other row, 3 times. Work even until armhole measures 7 inches (17.5 cm). Work across 11 (13, 15) stitches and place center 9 (11, 13) stitches on stitch holder. Join new yarn and work remaining 11 (13, 15) stitches. Decrease 1 stitch each neck edge 2 times. Work even until armhole measures 9 inches (22.5 cm), bind off.

Front

Work same as Back.

Sleeves

With #15 needles, cast on 20 (22, 22) stitches. Work in knit 1, purl 1 ribbing for 3 inches (7.5 cm). Change to #17 needles and work as follows:

Row 1: Knit across row.

Row 2: Knit 1, purl 1 across, increasing 1 stitch each side, every 4 inches (10 cm) 2 (2, 3) times, being sure to keep pattern as established. Work until sleeve measures 17 (18, 19) inches (42.5, 45, 47.5 cm) or desired length. At the beginning of the next 2 rows, bind off 2 stitches. Decrease 1 stitch each side, every other row, 7 (8, 8) times, and bind off remaining stitches.

Finishing

Sew shoulders together on one side. With right side of garment facing you, use #15 needles to pick up 40 (42, 44) stitches around neck, including stitches on holder. Work in knit 1, purl 1 ribbing for 3 rows. Bind off in ribbing pattern. Sew remaining shoulder and side seams. Sew sleeves and sew into armholes.

Man's Fisherman's Cable Cardigan

Man's Fisherman's Cable Cardigan
The cardigan version of the "weekend" fisherman cable pattern.

Men's Sizes
Directions are for small size. Changes for medium and large sizes are in parentheses.

Materials
9 (9, 10) skeins (3½ oz or 100 g each) Vail Homespun by Brunswick or any bulky yarn to give gauge
heavy-duty separating zipper

Needles
#15
#17
1 bulky double-pointed cable needle
2 large stitch holders

Gauge
2 stitches = 1 inch (2.5 cm)

Note: Yarn is worked double strand throughout.

Pattern
Row 1 (wrong side): *Knit 7 (9, 11), purl 1, knit 1, purl 6, knit 1, purl 1, repeat from * to last 7 (9, 11) stitches, knit to end of row.
Row 2 (right side): *Knit 1, purl 1 on first 7 (9, 11) stitches, knit 1, purl 1, knit 6, purl 1, knit 1, repeat from * to last 7 (9, 11) stitches, knit 1, purl 1 to end of row.
Row 3: Work same as Row 1.
Row 4 (cable row): *Knit 1, purl 1 on first 7 (9,11) stitches, knit 1, purl 1, slip next 3 stitches onto cable needle and hold in back of work, knit next 3 stitches, then knit the 3 stitches from cable needle, purl 1, knit 1, repeat from * to last 7 (9, 11) stitches, knit 1, purl 1 to end of row.
Row 5: Work same as Row 1.
Row 6: Work same as Row 2.
Row 7: Work same as Row 1.
Row 8: Work same as Row 2.

Back

With #15 needles, cast on 41 (47, 53) stitches. Work in knit 1, purl 1 ribbing for 3 inches (7.5 cm). Change to #17 needles and work the 8 rows of pattern until piece measures 16 inches (40 cm) or desired length from start to underarm, ending on wrong side. At the beginning of the next 2 rows, bind off 2 stitches. Decrease 1 stitch each side, every other row, 3 times. Work even until armhole measures 9 inches (22.5 cm). At the beginning of the next 2 rows, bind off 8 (8, 11) stitches. Bind off remaining stitches for back of neck.

Left Front

With #15 needles, cast on 24 (26, 28) stitches. Work in knit 1, purl 1 ribbing for 3 inches (7.5 cm). Change to #17 needles and work the 8 rows of pattern as on Back until piece measures 16 inches (40 cm) or same length as Back from start to underarm, end on wrong side. At the beginning of the next row, bind off 2 stitches. Decrease 1 stitch at arm side, every other row, 3 times. Work even until armhole measures 6 inches (15 cm), ending at front edge. Place 7 (9, 11) border stitches on stitch holder. Decrease 1 stitch at neck edge every other row, 4 times. Work even until armhole measures 9 inches (22.5 cm), bind off.

Right Front

Work same as Left Front, reversing all shaping.

Collar

Place the stitches that are on the holder back on #17 needle. Continue in pattern, increasing 1 stitch at inside edge every other row, 6 (7, 8) times. Work even until collar is 8 (9, 10) inches (20, 22.5, 25 cm) from last increase, bind off.

Sleeves

With #15 needles, cast on 20 (22, 22) stitches. Work in knit 1, purl 1 ribbing for 3 inches (7.5 cm). Change to #17 needles.
Row 1: Knit across row.
Row 2: Knit 1, purl 1 across, increasing 1 stitch each side, every 4 inches (10 cm), 2 (2, 3) times, being careful to keep pattern as established. (42.5, 45, 47.5 cm) or desired length. At the beginning of the next 2 rows, bind off 2 stitches. Decrease 1 stitch each side, every other row, 7 (8, 8) times, bind off remaining stitches.

Finishing

Sew shoulder seams and set in sleeves. Sew underarm seams. Join collar seam at back of neck and sew collar to sweater. Measure front from bottom of sweater to start of collar and sew in separating zipper.

Back view of Man's Fisherman Cable Cardigan.

Woman's Lacy Scarf

Sizes
One size

Materials
4 skeins (2 oz or 56 g each) Dji Dji by Stanley Berocco or any mohair yarn to give gauge

Needles
#13

Gauge
2 stitches = 1 inch (2.5 cm)

Pattern
Purl 1, *yarn over, purl 2 together, repeat from * across row.

Scarf
Cast on 40 stitches and work pattern for 72 inches (180 cm) or desired length, bind off.

Finishing
Tie several strands of yarn around scarf, about 10 inches (25 cm) up from each end. Do not block.

Woman's Lacy Scarf
Cast on 40 stitches, work the simple pattern for 72 inches, and you've got a lovely fashion accessory.

Index